10648319

Legalized Gambling

POINT | COUNTERPOINT

Legalized Gambling

Paul Ruschmann, J.D.

SERIES CONSULTING EDITOR
Alan Marzilli, M.A., J.D.

CHELSEA HOUSE
PUBLISHERS

An imprint of Infobase Publishing

NEW HANOVER COUNTY
PUBLIC LIBRARY
201 CHESTNUT STREET
WILMINTON, NC 28401

Legalized Gambling

Copyright © 2009 by Infobase Publishing

All rights reserved. No part of this book may be reproduced or utilized in any form or by any means, electronic or mechanical, including photocopying, recording, or by any information storage or retrieval systems, without permission in writing from the publisher. For information, contact:

Chelsea House
An imprint of Infobase Publishing
132 West 31st Street
New York NY 10001

Library of Congress Cataloging-in-Publication Data

Ruschmann, Paul.
  Legalized gambling / Paul Ruschmann.
    p. cm. — (Point/counterpoint series)
  Includes bibliographical references and index.
  ISBN 978-0-7910-9835-6 (hardcover)
  1. Gambling—Social aspects—United States. 2. Gambling—Economic aspects—United States. 3. Gambling—United States—States. I. Title.
  HV6715.R87 2008
  363.4'20973—dc22   2008027122

Chelsea House books are available at special discounts when purchased in bulk quantities for businesses, associations, institutions, or sales promotions. Please call our Special Sales Department in New York at (212) 967–8800 or (800) 322–8755.

You can find Chelsea House on the World Wide Web at
http://www.chelseahouse.com

Series design by Keith Trego
Cover design by Keith Trego and Jooyoung An

Printed in the United States of America

Bang NMSG 10 9 8 7 6 5 4 3 2 1

This book is printed on acid-free paper.

All links and Web addresses were checked and verified to be correct at the time of publication. Because of the dynamic nature of the Web, some addresses and links may have changed since publication and may no longer be valid.

Alan Marzilli, M.A., J.D.
Birmingham, Alabama

The POINT/COUNTERPOINT series offers the reader a greater understanding of some of the most controversial issues in contemporary American society—issues such as capital punishment, immigration, gay rights, and gun control. We have looked for the most contemporary issues and have included topics—such as the controversies surrounding "blogging"—that we could not have imagined when the series began.

In each volume, the author has selected an issue of particular importance and set out some of the key arguments on both sides of the issue. Why study both sides of the debate? Maybe you have yet to make up your mind on an issue, and the arguments presented in the book will help you to form an opinion. More likely, however, you will already have an opinion on many of the issues covered by the series. There is always the chance that you will change your opinion after reading the arguments for the other side. But even if you are firmly committed to an issue—for example, school prayer or animal rights—reading both sides of the argument will help you to become a more effective advocate for your cause. By gaining an understanding of opposing arguments, you can develop answers to those arguments.

Perhaps more importantly, listening to the other side sometimes helps you see your opponent's arguments in a more human way. For example, Sister Helen Prejean, one of the nation's most visible opponents of capital punishment, has been deeply affected by her interactions with the families of murder victims. By seeing the families' grief and pain, she understands much better why people support the death penalty, and she is able to carry out her advocacy with a greater sensitivity to the needs and beliefs of death penalty supporters.

The books in the series include numerous features that help the reader to gain a greater understanding of the issues. Real-life examples illustrate the human side of the issues. Each chapter also includes excerpts from relevant laws, court cases, and other material, which provide a better foundation for understanding the arguments. The volumes contain citations to relevant sources of law and information, and an appendix guides the reader through the basics of legal research, both on the Internet and in the library. Today, through free Web sites, it is easy to access legal documents, and these books might give you ideas for your own research.

Studying the issues covered by the POINT/COUNTERPOINT series is more than an academic activity. The issues described in the book affect all of us as citizens. They are the issues that today's leaders debate and tomorrow's leaders will decide. While all of the issues covered in the POINT/COUNTERPOINT series are controversial today, and will remain so for the foreseeable future, it is entirely possible that the reader might one day play a central role in resolving the debate. Today it might seem that some debates—such as capital punishment and abortion—will never be resolved.

However, our nation's history is full of debates that seemed as though they never would be resolved, and many of the issues are now well settled—at least on the surface. In the nineteenth century, abolitionists met with widespread resistance to their efforts to end slavery. Ultimately, the controversy threatened the union, leading to the Civil War between the northern and southern states. Today, while a public debate over the merits of slavery would be unthinkable, racism persists in many aspects of society.

Similarly, today nobody questions women's right to vote. Yet at the beginning of the twentieth century, suffragists fought public battles for women's voting rights, and it was not until the passage of the Nineteenth Amendment in 1920 that the legal right of women to vote was established nationwide.

What makes an issue controversial? Often, controversies arise when most people agree that there is a problem, but people disagree about the best way to solve the problem. There is little argument that poverty is a major problem in the United States, especially in inner cities and rural areas. Yet, people disagree vehemently about the best way to address the problem. To some, the answer is social programs, such as welfare, food stamps, and public housing. However, many argue that such subsidies encourage dependence on government benefits while unfairly penalizing those who work and pay taxes, and that the real solution is to require people to support themselves.

American society is in a constant state of change, and sometimes modern practices clash with what many consider to be "traditional values," which are often rooted in conservative political views or religious beliefs. Many blame high crime rates, and problems such as poverty, illiteracy, and drug use on the breakdown of the traditional family structure of a married mother and father raising their children. Since the "sexual revolution" of the 1960s and 1970s, sparked in part by the widespread availability of the birth control pill, marriage rates have declined, and the number of children born outside of marriage has increased. The sexual revolution led to controversies over birth control, sex education, and other issues, most prominently abortion. Similarly, the gay rights movement has been challenged as a threat to traditional values. While many gay men and lesbians want to have the same right to marry and raise families as heterosexuals, many politicians and others have challenged gay marriage and adoption as a threat to American society.

Sometimes, new technology raises issues that we have never faced before, and society disagrees about the best solution. Are people free to swap music online, or does this violate the copyright laws that protect songwriters and musicians' ownership of the music that they create? Should scientists use "genetic engineering" to create new crops that are resistant to disease and pests and produce more food, or is it too risky to use a laboratory to create plants that nature never intended? Modern medicine has continued to increase the average lifespan—which is now 77 years, up from under 50 years at the beginning of the twentieth century—but many people are now choosing to die in comfort rather than living with painful ailments in their later years. For doctors, this presents an ethical dilemma: should they allow their patients to die? Should they assist patients in ending their own lives painlessly?

Perhaps the most controversial issues are those that implicate a constitutional right. The Bill of Rights—the first 10 amendments to the U.S. Constitution—spell out some of the most fundamental rights that distinguish our democracy from other nations with fewer freedoms. However, the sparsely worded document is open to interpretation, with each side saying that the Constitution is on their side. The Bill of Rights was meant to protect individual liberties; however, the needs of some individuals clash with society's needs. Thus, the Constitution often serves as a battleground between individuals and government officials seeking to protect society in some way. The First Amendment's guarantee of "freedom of speech" leads to some very difficult questions. Some forms of expression—such as burning an American flag—lead to public outrage, but are protected by the First Amendment. Other types of expression that most people find objectionable—such as child pornography—are not protected by the Constitution. The question is not only where to draw the line, but whether drawing lines around constitutional rights threatens our liberty.

The Bill of Rights raises many other questions about individual rights and societal "good." Is a prayer before a high school football game an "establishment of religion" prohibited by the First Amendment? Does the Second Amendment's promise of "the right to bear arms" include concealed handguns? Does stopping and frisking someone standing on a known drug corner constitute "unreasonable search and seizure" in violation of the Fourth Amendment? Although the U.S. Supreme Court has the ultimate authority in interpreting the U.S. Constitution, its answers do not always satisfy the public. When a group of nine people—sometimes by a five-to-four vote—makes a decision that affects hundreds of millions of others, public outcry can be expected. For example, the Supreme Court's 1973 ruling in *Roe v. Wade* that abortion is protected by the Constitution did little to quell the debate over abortion.

Whatever the root of the controversy, the books in the POINT/ COUNTERPOINT series seek to explain to the reader the origins of the debate, the current state of the law, and the arguments on either side of the debate. Our hope in creating this series is that the reader will be better informed about the issues facing not only our politicians, but all of our nation's citizens, and become more actively involved in resolving these debates, as voters, concerned citizens, journalists, or maybe even elected officials.

This volume examines ongoing controversies relating to the legalization of gambling. The issues are complex, in part because there are so many forms of gambling, each of which has varying levels of public acceptance. People are more likely to approve of church raffles, poker nights among friends, and office basketball tournament brackets—all technically illegal—than they are of betting with sports bookies. Further complicating matters, the issues are being debated not only by the federal government and the individual states, but also by Native American tribes, which have limited authority under federal law to establish casinos.

Many Americans oppose gambling on moral grounds or point to the problems faced by "compulsive gamblers," who are unable to stop even as their debts mount. Yet, millions of Americans gamble, both legally and illegally. Legalized gambling has boomed in the past few decades. Once confined to Nevada and Atlantic City, New Jersey, casinos now operate in a number of states, and can be found on Native American reservations in states where casino gambling is otherwise illegal. Including state-run lotteries, almost every state has some form of legalized gambling. At the same time, illegal gambling has also boomed, fueled in part by the Internet.

With a patchwork of laws across the nation, some say that the government should stop regulating an activity that many people enjoy, while others warn that we have gone too far in approving an immoral and harmful activity. Particularly controversial is the question of whether the government should sponsor gambling through lotteries. Even in states in which there is strong, organized opposition to lotteries, it can be difficult for legislators to resist the lure of lottery money. It is even more difficult when nearby states have lotteries that can draw players' money across the border. Although the trend has been toward legalizing more forms of gambling, the federal government's efforts to crack down on Internet gambling could signal a swing in the pendulum.

Gambling in the United States

The words *gambling* and *gaming* are both used to describe "an activity in which something of value is risked on the chance that something of greater value might be obtained, based on the uncertain outcome of a particular event."[1] The word *gaming*, which can be traced back to *gamen*, the Old English word for "game," once described betting on games such as cards and dice. Later, opponents to the practice coined the term *gambling*, which reflected their disapproval.

The use of two different words to describe the same activity reflects a deep and long-standing controversy over its acceptability. Since early colonial days, U.S. laws have swung between prohibition and outright acceptance. Today, some form of gambling is legal in almost every state, and most people take part in it, at least on occasion. Gambling has become a huge and profitable industry.

Gambling: The American Pastime

As early as 1566, England's royal family held a lottery to cover some of its expenses. The English colonists who arrived in what is now the United States soon copied the practice. Robert Goodman, a professor at Hampshire College, writes, "In this country, public and private lotteries have existed, off and on, since earliest colonial times. When the Virginia Company, the English enterprise that financed that country's first American settlement in Jamestown, fell on hard times, it resorted to selling lottery tickets in England to sustain its military and other expenses in the New World."[2] In the early days of the republic, the banking system was primitive and the government imposed only a handful of taxes. As a result, public officials turned to lotteries to pay for public works projects such as roads, bridges, and canals. Lotteries raised funds for the Continental Army during the Revolutionary War, and helped build the universities of Harvard and Yale. Lotteries were even used to dispose of large parcels of real estate.

From the beginning, many colonists had moral objections to gambling. Jackson Lears, a professor at Rutgers University, observes, "Beginning in 1621, when King James I told Governor Francis Wyatt of Virginia that the drunkenness and gambling at Jamestown must be suppressed, colonial officials fretted about the impact of gambling on the social fabric and attempted to control it with legislation."[3] The Puritans, who settled much of New England, opposed gambling because it undermined the "Protestant ethic" of self-control, hard work, and thrift. Religious leaders condemned gambling because they believed that it destroyed families and communities and exposed gamblers to other vices, such as alcohol abuse and prostitution. There was so much opposition to gambling in seventeenth-century Massachusetts that lawmakers passed laws against playing cards and dice, and even shuffleboard and bowling. Other colonies cracked down on gambling as well. Virginia outlawed gambling on Sundays, later allowed gamblers to recover their losses in court, and ultimately banned gambling altogether.

Lotteries reached their height of popularity in the 1830s, but then quickly fell out of favor. Richard Hoffer, a writer for *Sports Illustrated*, described what happened: "[A] religious and legal backlash began to form. The fever led to rampant privatization and inevitable corruption and was not counterbalanced by the feel-good effect of better highways and schools. By 1860, a lottery backlash had put all but three states out of business."[4]

The Pendulum Swings

After the Civil War, states in the South turned to lotteries as a means of rebuilding their economies. The best-known game from that era was the Louisiana Lottery, whose promoters sold tickets across the country. It was the ancestor of today's Mega Millions and Powerball games. The Louisiana Lottery was plagued by corruption, which again fueled public opposition. By the end of the century, Congress made it illegal to mail lottery tickets across state lines, and lotteries were outlawed in every state.

Further opposition came later, for reasons not based on religion. Jackson Lears relates one example:

> During the 1890s, German socialists in Saint Louis objected to slot machines in working-men's saloons for a variety of reasons: the machines preyed on the poor; they discouraged education, self-development, and upward mobility among the working class; and they offered reformers an excuse to shut down all recreational watering-holes.[5]

Reformers of the early twentieth century believed that the government should make society safer and cleaner. They passed laws aimed at ridding politics of bribery and corruption, at keeping dangerous products and worthless drugs off the market, and at improving sanitation and housing in the cities. They also legislated against "vices" such as liquor. The result was near-prohibition of gambling:

> By 1910, legal or illegal gambling had hit a low ebb, rarely matched before in our history. Horse racing survived in Kentucky, Maryland, and a few other select locations—though even New York banned the sport from 1910 to 1913. On the frontier, antigambling campaigns achieved unprecedented gains. At least for a while, the forces of systematic self-control sustained the compliance of a majority.[6]

Laws did not stop people from gambling. That was especially true in cities with large immigrant populations. Gambling historian Mark Heller noted that from the 1880s until about 1905, gamblers exercised an influence on local politics and law enforcement that has seldom been equaled since. In some neighborhoods, gambling syndicates *were* the local political organization.

Legalized Gambling Returns

In 1931, Nevada once again legalized casinos in an effort to revive the state's stagnant economy. In doing so, lawmakers conceded that gambling prohibition had failed. People still gambled, only now organized crime ran gambling. After legalization, the laws controlling gambling created another set of problems. Many of the founding investors of Las Vegas's casino industry, such as Bugsy Siegel and Meyer Lansky, were underworld figures who had made their fortunes selling bootleg liquor during Prohibition. Even after federal authorities cracked down on them, organized crime ran some casinos from behind the scenes.

At the same time, other forms of gambling gained acceptance. Bingo became popular, especially in areas with a large population of Roman Catholics, whose faith did not consider social gambling a sin. Many Catholic parishes and a variety of charitable organizations held bingo games to raise funds. Even in states where bingo was illegal, authorities rarely interfered with the games.

Some states also legalized wagering on horse races. One major reason was *pari-mutuel wagering*: "Odds were set automatically, by combining all bets in a common pool and playing off the amounts bet on each horse against the amounts bet on the others; the horse with the most bettors had the shortest odds."[7] This practice made the races more honest. Perhaps more importantly, pari-mutuel betting made it easier for states to collect taxes from racetracks. Even some lawmakers who disapproved of gambling on principle believed that regulating horse racing and taxing the racetracks was a lesser evil than continuing to let bookmakers take illegal wagers and keep the profits for themselves.

Still, many officials believed that legalization was not a cure-all for the problems associated with gambling. They had reason to be concerned. In 1950 and 1951, a committee led by Senator Estes Kefauver investigated the extent to which organized crime had infiltrated legitimate businesses. The committee found that crime families had established themselves in Nevada's legal gaming industry and had bribed public officials elsewhere to "look the other way" when it came to illegal gambling. Congress responded by passing new laws aimed at organized crime, and federal authorities tried to stamp out illegal gambling in order to deprive the underworld of a major source of its money.

States Enter the Gambling Business

After years of being illegal, the lottery reappeared in 1964 in New Hampshire. Lawmakers there turned to a lottery to raise money because voters were opposed to paying a sales tax or an income tax. The state tried to soften public aversion to lotteries by calling the game a "sweepstakes" and promising that lottery revenue would go to the schools. New Hampshire's lottery was modest by today's standards: The top prize was $100,000, and there were

States bet on gambling measures

Six states have gambling initiatives on their Nov. 2 ballot. The most contentious boil down to non-tribal versus tribal gambling.

States with legalized gambling*

Tribal and non-tribal casinos

Tribal casinos

Non-tribal casinos

Other non-casino gambling

States with gambling-related ballot measures

* May also include charitable bingo, card rooms, sports betting and racetracks

SOURCE: National Conference of State Legislatures   AP

The graphic above shows the various kinds of legalized gambling throughout the United States. Some states allow only tribal gambling—that is, gambling at facilities located on Native American reservations, which are not subject to the same gambling rules as the rest of the state.

only two drawings a year. Lotteries became popular after New Jersey, which started its lottery in 1970, offered cheaper tickets, made them easier to buy, and held more frequent drawings with bigger prizes. In the years that followed, lotteries spread to other states. Today, 41 states and the District of Columbia have them.

The New Hampshire Lottery is significant for two reasons: First, it brought the government itself into the gambling business. That business grew as lottery officials introduced instant tickets, multistate lotto games with huge jackpots, and in some states, casino-style games such as slot machines, video poker, and keno. According to the North American Association of State and Provincial Lotteries, Americans bought $53.2 billion worth of tickets during fiscal year 2005. Second, New Hampshire's lottery ushered in an era of widespread legal gambling. Americans no longer need to drive to a racetrack or fly to Las Vegas to gamble. In many parts of the country, a person can place a bet in his or her own neighborhood.

Casino Gaming Spreads

In 1978, high-stakes casino gaming spread beyond Nevada when the first casino opened in Atlantic City, a seaside resort that had fallen on hard times. After that, a number of states legalized gaming (the term preferred by the casino industry) on riverboats, in historic towns, and more recently, in urban areas.

In many states, however, casino gaming did not arrive because of a vote of the people, but rather as the unintended result of a legal dispute between Native American tribes and the states over bingo. It began when the Seminoles of Florida offered much bigger jackpots than state law allowed. The state sued, but in *Seminole Tribe of Florida v. Butterworth*, a federal appeals court ruled that the Seminoles were a sovereign nation and therefore not subject to Florida's bingo laws. After that decision, tribes elsewhere opened their own bingo halls and state officials fought them in court. The issue finally came before the U.S. Supreme Court in *California v. Cabazon Band of Mission Indians*. In that case, the justices had to determine California's policy toward bingo. Since California allowed bingo as well as several other forms of gambling, the justices reasoned that the state intended to regulate gambling rather than prohibit it. Because California merely regulated bingo, the court ruled that it could not shut down games on tribal lands. The upshot of the *Cabazon* decision was that if a state allowed a form of gambling anywhere within its borders, it could not outlaw the same form of gambling on Native American lands.

Congress reacted to the *Cabazon* decision by passing the Indian Gaming Regulatory Act of 1988 (IGRA).[8] IGRA's primary intent was to establish ground rules for tribal bingo games. It permitted a tribe to build a bingo hall if the state allowed bingo elsewhere, and if a new federal regulatory body called the National Indian Gaming Commission (NIGC) found that the games would be honestly run. Criminals therefore could not infiltrate the gaming operation, and the revenue would go back to the tribe.

IGRA also contained a huge legal loophole. It allowed tribes to offer casino-type games if the state where the tribe is located "permits such gaming for any purpose by any person, organization, or entity."[9] Lawyers for the tribes argued successfully that if a state legalized "Las Vegas nights," where people played low-stakes games of blackjack, craps, and roulette for charity, the tribe had the right to build a full-fledged casino on its land.

Today, 30 states have tribal casinos, commercial casinos, or both. According to the American Gaming Association, commercial casinos earned $31.85 billion in 2005, while tribal gaming, which includes both casinos and bingo halls, earned $22.6 billion.

Too Much Too Soon?

When legalized, often high-stakes gambling became more widely available. Many Americans believed that it had become too easy for people, especially young people, to bet irresponsibly—even to the point of harming themselves and those close to them. In 1980, the American Psychiatric Association (APA) officially recognized a disorder known as *compulsive gambling*.[10] Scientists believe that millions of Americans either are compulsive gamblers or will develop the disorder during their lifetime.

Indian Gaming Upheld: *California v. Cabazon Band of Mission Indians*

The U.S. Supreme Court has repeatedly ruled that Native American tribes are distinct and independent political communities with broad power to govern themselves. This so-called *tribal sovereignty* includes the right to engage in economic activity on tribal lands without interference by state officials. Native American communities are, however, subject to federal law. The court has recognized that the federal government has a unique obligation to look after the tribes' interests.

Beginning in the 1970s, some Native American tribes tried to raise money by opening bingo halls in states where bingo was legal. A few decided to offer larger jackpots than state law allowed, defying the law on the grounds that since they were sovereign nations, the prize limits did not apply. A test case arose in Florida when the state tried to stop the Miami Seminole tribe from offering games with $10,000 jackpots. The U.S. Court of Appeals for the Fifth Circuit ruled in the tribe's favor in *Seminole Tribe of Florida v. Butterworth*, 658F.2d310 (5th Cir. 1981). Tribes in other states began to offer high-stakes bingo. By the mid 1980s, there were more than 100 bingo halls across the country. The states, however, continued to fight the tribes in court.

The issue of tribal bingo eventually came before the U.S. Supreme Court. The case of *California v. Cabazon Band of Mission Indians*, 480 U.S. 202 (1987), began when the Cabazon and Morongo bands of Mission Indians, two federally recognized tribes who lived on reservations in California, opened bingo halls. The state tried to shut down the bingo halls on the grounds that the tribes offered larger jackpots than allowed by state law and used paid employees to run the games. The tribes went to court, arguing that California had no authority to enforce its bingo laws on their land. Both the trial court and appeals court ruled in the tribes' favor. The state appealed to the U.S. Supreme Court, which, by a 6 to 3 vote, ruled in favor of the tribes.

Justice Byron White wrote the majority opinion. Citing past Supreme Court decisions, he stated the general principle that on Native American reservations, states could not enforce laws that were civil, rather than criminal, in nature. The test, he said, was whether the overall purpose of the law was to regulate an activity rather than prohibit it. In this case, Justice White found that California regulated gambling but did not prohibit it altogether. He pointed out that the state operated a lottery and allowed several of forms of gambling, including bingo, and that bingo games were sponsored by a variety of organizations and widely played by Californians. He wrote, "In light of the fact that California permits a substantial amount of gambling activity, including bingo, and actually promotes gambling through its state lottery, we must conclude that California regulates, rather than prohibits, gambling in general and bingo in particular."

Justice White next concluded that gaming on Native American reservations was consistent with federal policy. He noted that federal authorities had not only allowed tribes to offer bingo but also encouraged them to do so. In fact, the government even provided financial aid to tribes who wanted to build bingo halls. Justice White added that bingo promoted the welfare of the Cabazon and Morongo tribes, who lived on barren land with no natural resources and thus had to turn to bingo in order to become self-sufficient.

Justice White also concluded that the tribes were doing more than merely taking advantage of a legal loophole. He wrote:

> Here, however, the Tribes are not merely importing a product onto the reservations for immediate resale to non-Indians. They have built modern facilities which provide recreational opportunities and ancillary services to their patrons, who do not simply drive onto the reservations, make purchases and depart, but spend extended periods of time there enjoying the services the Tribes provide.

He rejected California's contention that it had to enforce its bingo laws on tribal lands in order to curb organized crime. He found that the federal and tribal interests in offering bingo outweighed the state's interests in regulating it, and that California had offered no evidence that organized crime had infiltrated the tribes' bingo games.

Justice John Paul Stevens dissented. He wrote: "Unless and until Congress exempts Indian-managed gambling from state law and subjects it to federal supervision, I believe that a State may enforce its laws prohibiting high-stakes gambling on Indian reservations within its borders." He also warned: "Accepting the majority's reasoning would require exemptions for cockfighting, tattoo parlors, nude dancing, houses of prostitution, and other illegal but profitable enterprises." Justice Stevens pointed out that the commercial transactions in this case were between Indians and non-Indians, which had never enjoyed blanket immunity from state regulation, and found it "painfully obvious" that the tribes' exemption from state law was the primary attraction to non-Indians who otherwise would have gambled elsewhere. He also argued that California had reason to be concerned that unregulated, high-stakes bingo games could be infiltrated by organized crime.

Opponents of legalized gambling argue that the costs of compulsive gambling are unacceptably high, and that gambling adds nothing of value to the economy.

Congress reacted to growing concern over gambling by creating the National Gambling Impact Study Commission. In 1999, the commission released its report, recommending that policymakers consider "a pause in the expansion of gambling" in order "to encourage governments to do what to date few if any have done: To survey the results of their decisions and to determine if they have chosen wisely."[11] The commission also

The Wire Act

After the Kefauver Commission found that organized crime had a substantial presence in illegal gambling, Congress passed a series of laws aimed at driving them out of business. Perhaps the most important such law was the Interstate Wire Act of 1961, which was directed at illegal bookmakers who took bets on horse races and sporting events. Section 1084(a) provides:

Whoever being engaged in the business of betting or wagering knowingly uses a wire communication facility for the transmission in interstate or foreign commerce of bets or wagers or information assisting in the placing of bets or wagers on any sporting event or contest, or for the transmission of a wire communication which entitles the recipient to receive money or credit as a result of bets or wagers, or for information assisting in the placing of bets or wagers, shall be fined under this title or imprisoned not more than two years, or both.

The Wire Act was passed before the Internet even existed. After casinos went online, legal experts identified several issues that could arise if federal authorities tried to use the law against casino Web sites:

* Offshore gambling Web sites might not be under U.S. jurisdiction.

* Internet service providers (ISPs) might not fall within the definition of "wire communications facilities."

* The law specifically mentions only sports betting and does not mention casino gaming.

called for measures that would make gambling less accessible to young people, compulsive gamblers, and the poor.

Gambling in the Internet Era

In spite of the commission's recommendations, legalized gambling has continued to spread. The Internet allows people to place bets from their homes, and this has become a major concern. Online gambling is difficult to regulate because the Internet makes it easier for money to cross state and even national boundaries. A number of countries allow gambling Web sites

- It is hard for the government to prove that an online gambling site "knowingly" transmits bets from Americans because the physical location of online gamblers cannot be determined.

In spite of these concerns, the Wire Act was, for years, the federal government's principal legal tool in pursuing online casinos.

Congress considered, but did not pass, legislation that would regulate online gambling per se. The Internet Gambling Prohibition Act of 1997 would have banned gambling Web sites altogether, and would have made it a crime for an American to place a bet online. At first, land-based casinos endorsed a complete ban because online casinos would compete with them. (The gaming industry no longer supports a ban, and many observers believe that it would like to establish an online presence.) Opponents of the bill included Native American tribes who wanted to run online lotteries, and ISPs that feared the law would place too much of an administrative burden on them.

In 1999, a milder version of the Internet Gambling Prohibition Act was introduced. It did not apply to individual bettors, and also contained exemptions for state lotteries, pari-mutuel racing, and fantasy sports leagues. The legislation was kept from passing due in large part to the efforts of Jack Abramoff, a powerful lobbyist who represented a business that wanted to operate an online lottery. It would take seven more years for Congress to pass the first law directed at online gambling.

to operate within their boundaries. Even though those Web sites are located abroad, they advertise on media that reach Americans rather than local residents.

THE LETTER OF THE LAW

The Unlawful Internet Gambling Enforcement Act of 2006

The National Gambling Impact Study Commission recognized that online gambling had become a problem: The Internet has made it easier for young people and compulsive gamblers to place bets; gambling Web sites could be used to hide the source of ill-gotten money, such as the proceeds of illegal drug sales; and players could be cheated by dishonest Web site operators. The commission recommended that Congress pass legislation that prohibited banks and other card issuers from transferring money to gambling sites.

In 2006, Congress passed a criminal statute called the Unlawful Internet Gambling Enforcement Act (UIGEA). This law did not expand the Wire Act to online gambling, as some advocates had proposed, nor did it make it illegal for Americans to place a bet online. What UIGEA did instead was make it harder for bettors to transfer their money to gambling Web sites.

UIGEA focuses on owners and operators of *illegal* gambling sites. Its definition of "bet or wager" (§5362(1)(E)) exempts the trading of stocks, bonds, commodities, or financial instruments; contests in which participants risk nothing of value; and fantasy sports leagues. In addition, §5362(10)(B) exempts gambling that:

(i)   Does not cross state lines;

(ii)   Is authorized by state law (for example, California allows its residents to bet on horse races online); and

(iii)   Is already allowed under federal law (for example, betting on "simulcasts" of horse races at licensed sports books in Nevada or at authorized Indian casinos.)

The law, therefore, is directed at online casinos, sports books, and interactive poker sites that operate outside the United States and offer forms of gambling that are illegal in the United States.

Section 5363 defines what UIGEA prohibits. It bars a person who is "engaged in the business of betting or wagering" from knowingly accepting any of the following in connection with illegal Internet gambling:

The legal status of online gambling is somewhat unsettled. At the federal level, there is no law that forbids Americans to bet online, nor is there a specific ban on online gambling sites. So

(1) Credit extended on a credit card;

(2) An electronic funds transfer, or funds transmitted using a money transmitting business;

(3) A check or similar instrument; or

(4) Funds resulting from any other transaction in which a financial institution is making payment.

Thus, the UIGEA bars illegal gambling Web sites from accepting most forms of funds that bettors use. Even though Web sites are the UIGEA's primary target, §5367 provides that a financial transaction provider, an Internet service provider (ISP), or a telecommunications company is liable if it owns or operates a gambling Web site and knows that gambling is occurring there.

The UIGEA's definition of "financial transaction provider" (§5362(4)) includes a creditor; a credit card issuer; a financial institution; the operator of a terminal where electronic funds transfers take place; a money transmitting business; and a payment network that is used "to effect a credit transaction, electronic fund transfer, stored value product transaction, or money transmitting service, or a participant in such network, or other participant in a designated payment system." Legal experts believe that this definition is broad enough to apply to offshore intermediaries such as NETeller.

Section 5634 requires financial institutions to adopt procedures designed to identify and stop transfers of funds to gambling Web sites. It also provides that a financial institution cannot be held liable for having acted in good faith to stop such a transfer.

Section 5365 authorizes federal and state attorneys general to ask a court to stop the transfer of funds to a gambling Web site or to "take down" (deny access to) an illegal gambling Web site or a Web site that links to it. However, that section also provides that a court may not force an ISP to look for illegal gambling Web sites.

Section 5366 makes a UIGEA violation punishable by up to five years in prison. A person who aids or abets a violation can be punished as well. That section also gives a federal court the power to permanently bar a person convicted under UIGEA from placing or taking bets.

far, federal authorities have relied on the Interstate Wire Act of 1961 (Wire Act),[12] a law originally aimed at sports betting over the telephone, to pursue operators of gambling Web sites. The courts have generally ruled that the Wire Act applies to online "sports books" but not casinos. In 2006, after years of debate, Congress passed the Unlawful Internet Gambling Enforcement Act (UIGEA).[13] It was the first law directed specifically at online gambling. UIGEA discourages online gambling by forbidding financial institutions, such as credit card companies, to do business with illegal gambling Web sites. After the law passed, popular Web sites suffered a significant loss of business. Many observers believe that UIGEA has discouraged casual gamblers from playing online, but suspect that some hardcore gamblers have the money and technical know-how to evade the law's restrictions.

Online gambling raises new legal issues, such as how far the United States can go in enforcing its laws against people and businesses located in other countries. It also raises practical issues, such as whether laws can stop Americans from placing bets online. Some argue that laws against online gambling are a new form of Prohibition and urge the government to legalize and regulate it, just as it did with horse racing, the lottery, and land-based casinos.

Summary

Millions of Americans enjoy gambling, but many believe that it leads to antisocial behavior. U.S. laws reflect this long-standing conflict over gambling. Over the years they have alternated between near-prohibition and the current policy of legalization. In recent decades, however, three events triggered widespread gambling: the lottery brought states into the gambling business, and gambling into neighborhoods; the *Cabazon* decision paved the way for tribal gaming in many states; and the Internet made it possible to place a bet from one's home. Many believe that the move to legalize gambling came too quickly and that lawmakers should take a second look at the policies behind it.

Gambling Is Harmful to Society

I n 2006, a Harris Interactive poll found that public approval of legalized gambling had fallen off since a 1989 Gallup survey. The Harris poll reported a 7 percent decline in approval for the lottery as well as declines of 9 percent for bingo, 4 percent for off-track betting, and 3 percent for casino gaming. The survey attributed the erosion of public support to increased concern that people are gambling with money they do not have. The poll numbers suggest more generally that Americans are becoming more aware of the social and economic costs of legalized gambling: Studies show that many Americans are either pathological gamblers or at risk of becoming one. The effects of pathological gambling go beyond the gamblers themselves. Their families, employers, and in some cases, other members of the community are affected as well.

Gambling has become more pervasive.

In 1976, the U.S. Commission on the Review of the National Policy Toward Gambling recommended that "any legalization of casino gambling be restricted by the State to relatively isolated areas where the impact on surrounding populations can be minimized."[14] In recent years, however, hundreds of commercial and tribal casinos have opened across the United States. Some of them are even located in or near major cities such as Chicago, Detroit, and New Orleans.

The nature of gambling has changed as well. Fifty years ago, a day at the racetrack was a popular form of gambling. The pace of betting was leisurely, and a person could wager as little as two dollars that a horse would finish at least third. (To this day, racetracks accept two-dollar bets.) Bingo was also popular. The proceeds of that went to charity, and the gambling was primarily a social activity: "People in lower income groups tended to play bingo, spending an average of less than $6 per session for the thrill of the games. Most played just to have a good time, and bingo parlors were famously sociable places where winners basked in praise and losers confronted each other."[15]

Modern-day gambling has little in common with horse racing or bingo. Eleven states have legalized "racinos"—that is, slot machines at racetracks. In some states, it is legal to play casino-type games in adult establishments such as bars. Other states allow slot machines and video poker games in truck stops and convenience stores.

The National Gambling Impact Study Commission (NGISC) concluded that "convenience gambling," the intrusion of electronic games into towns and neighborhoods, was the most destructive form of gambling because it generated social and economic costs but offered no offsetting benefits. In its final report, the commission observed:

Robert Hunter, a clinical psychologist in Las Vegas who specializes in problem and pathological gambling, calls electronic gambling devices "the distilled essence of gambling." He claims that video poker's hold on people is caused by the game's rapid pace (an experienced player can play 12 hands a minute), the ability to play for long periods of time, and the mesmerizing effect of music and rapidly flashing lights. Of problem and pathological gamblers who use these machines, Hunter says, "They sort of escape into the machine and make the world go away. It's like a trip to the Twilight Zone."[16]

The fast pace of today's games has increased the risk of problem gambling. In one study, researchers at Brown University found that it took an average of 3.58 years for a person who played "traditional" games to become a pathological gambler. It only took an average of 1.08 years for a person who played gambling machines. Vicki Abt and her co-authors at Brown explain why these games are so dangerous: "The more aggressive forms of gambling stimulate behaviors that progressively extend these limits [of how much a person will spend] and may, for some percentage of the population, erase them entirely."[17] Some gambling addiction experts warn that the Internet makes it easier yet for players to develop gambling problems because their gambling is no longer social. According to the Council on Compulsive Gaming of New Jersey, an estimated 90 to 95 percent of online gamblers play by themselves.

Legalization encourages problem and underage gambling.

In 1975, researchers at the University of Michigan found that 0.77 percent of American adults were "probable" compulsive gamblers and 2.33 percent were "potential" compulsive gamblers. The expansion of legal gambling has apparently made the problem worse. The NGISC found that in the 1990s, the compulsive gambling population had grown by at least 50 percent, to at least 1.2 percent of American adults—and that estimate was based on the most conservative study relied upon by the

Important Dates In American Gambling History

1612 King James I of England approves a lottery to support the Virginia Company's colony at Jamestown.

1777 The Continental Congress votes to authorize a lottery to help pay the costs of the Revolutionary War.

1832 The popularity of lotteries reaches a peak. Afterward, lottery-related scandals fuel a movement to ban them. By the beginning of the Civil War, all but a handful of states have legislated lotteries out of existence.

1890 In an effort to shut down Louisiana's lottery, Congress bans lottery materials from the U.S. mail. Louisiana's lottery goes out of business in 1892.

1891 New York becomes the first state to regulate horse racing by creating a licensing system for jockeys and trainers. Two decades later, New York bows to antigambling sentiment and briefly closes its racetracks.

1910s to 1920s Legalized gaming is practically nonexistent in the United States.

1931 Nevada relegalizes casino gaming.

1935 Several states legalize pari-mutuel wagering on horse races.

1945 Las Vegas licenses its first casino.

1950 to 1951 A committee led by Senator Estes Kefauver launches a congressional investigation of organized crime in the United States. The senators find that the underworld had infiltrated Las Vegas casinos and was a force behind illegal gambling elsewhere.

1957 Two problem gamblers establish the first Gamblers Anonymous chapter in Los Angeles.

1964 Lotteries return to the United States when New Hampshire sells the first ticket for its state-run game. New York (1967) and New Jersey (1970) are the next two states to offer a lottery.

1971 New York legalizes off-track betting (OTB).

1972 New Jersey creates the first daily lottery.

1974 The Massachusetts Lottery offers the first instant tickets.

1975 Congress repeals the federal ban on lottery advertising.

1976 New Jersey voters approve casino gaming in Atlantic City. The first casino opens two years later.

1980 The American Psychiatric Association recognizes pathological gambling as a mental disorder.

1982   North Dakota legalizes small-stakes, casino-type games, with proceeds going to charity.

1985   Montana becomes the first state outside Nevada to legalize slot machines in bars.

1987   In *California v. Cabazon Band of Mission Indians*, the U.S. Supreme Court rules that states cannot prohibit Native American tribes from offering gaming that is legal elsewhere in the state.

1988   Congress passes the Indian Gaming Regulatory Act. Tribes in 28 states have taken advantage of the law and built either casinos or bingo halls on their land.

The first multistate lottery game begins operations.

1989   Iowa legalizes low-stakes gaming ($5 per bet, $200 in losses per day) on riverboats. The first riverboat casino opens in 1991. In the years that follow, several other states in the region offer riverboat gambling. Faced with out-of-state competition, Iowa lawmakers repeal the limit on bets.

South Dakota legalizes video lottery terminals in bars and convenience stores. That same year, voters legalize low-stakes ($5 per bet) casino gaming in the town of Deadwood. In 2000, the bet limit is raised to $100.

1991   Colorado legalizes low-stakes casino gaming in three historic mining towns. The maximum bet is still $5.

1992   Congress passes the Professional and Amateur Sports Protection Act, which bans sports betting outside Nevada.

The first "racino," or racetrack casino, opens in Rhode Island.

1995   Interactive Casinos, Inc., said to be the first online casino, begins taking bets.

1996   Michigan voters approve casino gaming in downtown Detroit. The first casino opens three years later.

1997   Congress considers, but does not pass, the Internet Gambling Prohibition Act. The law would have imposed criminal penalties on Americans who bet online.

1999   The National Gambling Impact Study Commission releases its final report. It calls for a "pause" on the expansion of legalized gambling until its effects can be studied.

2006   Congress passes the Unlawful Internet Gambling Enforcement Act, the first law aimed at online gambling. The law does not ban Americans from placing bets, but makes it more difficult to do so by forbidding financial institutions to do business with online casinos.

commission. In Nevada, which has the nation's most liberal gambling laws, a 2000 study report found that pathological gamblers made up 3.5 percent of the state population.

Gambling opponents argue that closer proximity to gambling increases the risk of addiction. The NGISC cited a study noting that people who lived within 50 miles of a casino ran twice the risk of developing a gambling problem as those living farther away. Multiple forms of legal gambling also might increase the number of problem gamblers. Researchers at the University of Minnesota Duluth found that the percentage of pathological and problem gambling in Minnesota increased from 2.5 percent in 1990 to 4.4 percent in 1994. That increase coincided with the creation of the Minnesota State Lottery and a large increase in the number of tribal casinos in the state.

Young people are at an especially high risk of developing gambling problems. As *Time* magazine senior writer Jeffrey Kluger noted, "Exact figures aren't easy to come by, but various studies place the rate of problem gambling among underage players somewhere between two and three times the rate for adults."[18] This is especially disturbing because the American Psychiatric Association (APA) has found that compulsive gambling tends to begin in males during their teenage years—and males account for two-thirds of those with the disorder. The spread of legal gambling to places such as truck stops, convenience stores, and even supermarkets increases the likelihood that young people will place bets—even if they are too young to do so legally. The NGISC cited a survey of 12,000 teenagers in Louisiana, in which one-quarter reported that they had played video poker, 17 percent had played slot machines, and 10 percent had bet on a horse or dog race. The Internet is an important contributing factor as well. "If left unchecked, the growth of Internet gambling may be fueled by college students." Bill Saum, an official at the National Collegiate Athletic Association (NCAA), told a congressional committee. "After all, who else has greater access to the Internet?"[19]

Gambling breeds crime and other social problems.

One apparent result of legalized gambling is more crime. Jeffrey Bloomberg, a prosecuting attorney in South Dakota, told a congressional panel about the effects of casino gaming in the town of Deadwood:

> I think of the pizza restaurant manager who had a spotless record and embezzled $45,000 from his employers . . . or the gaming business bookkeeper who, having run up thousands in debt, committed suicide; or, most tragically, the technical sergeant in the United States Air Force, who prior to gaming had an exemplary 10-year military career, and who became hooked on slot machines and eventually murdered a casino operator in a desperate attempt to retrieve $400 in bad checks he had written to the casino.[20]

Communities with legal gambling suffer from higher crime rates. "Three years after the introduction of casinos, there was a tripling of total crimes. Per capita crime in Atlantic City jumped from fiftieth in the nation to first,"[21] notes writer Carl Bechtold. And Nevada, where casino gaming is most concentrated, has the nation's highest rate of serious crime, Bechtold says. Theft is a common gambling-related crime because many losing gamblers go heavily into debt. Senator Paul Simon, an opponent of legalized gambling, cited a study conducted by the insurance industry suggesting that 40 percent of white-collar crime could be traced to gambling. Most of those offenders had no prior criminal record.

Problem gambling leads to other social problems, such as bankruptcy. In a study commissioned by the banking industry, SMR Research Corporation found in the late 1990s that legalized gambling was not only the fastest-growing cause but also the third major cause of individual bankruptcies in the United States.

Another problem rooted in gambling addiction is child neglect. Jeffrey Bloomberg told federal lawmakers:

[Problems] run the spectrum from the children left in their cars all night while their parents gamble, to the children left at home alone while their parents gamble, to the children left at home alone while single mothers work the casino

Defining "Problem" and "Pathological" Gamblers

In 1980, the American Psychiatric Association (APA) officially recognized *pathological gambling* as a mental disorder and, for the first time, added it to its diagnostic manual.

Section 312.31 of the manual deals with pathological gambling. The APA called the disorder "extremely incapacitating" because those who suffer from it run the risk of losing all their money and their ability to support themselves and their family. Pathological gamblers also might become alienated from family and acquaintances and lose what they have attained in life. Pathological gambling is "progressive," which means that as time goes on, a person who has the disorder tends to bet more often and in larger amounts and becomes increasingly preoccupied with gambling and finding money with which to gamble.

Scientists have found that men make up about two-thirds of the compulsive gambling population. Women are less likely to seek treatment, perhaps because there is a greater stigma attached to female gamblers. Pathological gambling typically begins in the early teen years in males and later in life in females.

According to the APA's diagnostic criteria,* pathological gambling is defined as "persistent and recurrent maladaptive gambling behavior" as indicated by five or more of the following:

1. Preoccupation with gambling, for example, reliving past gambling experiences, handicapping upcoming events, planning the next venture, or thinking of ways to get money with which to gamble.
2. The need to bet increasing amounts of money in order to achieve the desired excitement.
3. Repeated unsuccessful efforts to control, cut back, or stop gambling.

late shift, to the household without utilities or groceries because one or both parents have blown their paycheck gambling.[22]

Gambling opponents have also linked legalized gambling to drug and alcohol abuse, job loss, domestic violence, broken families, and even suicide.

4. Restlessness or irritability when attempting to cut down or stop gambling.
5. Using gambling as a way to escape from problems or to relieve feelings of helplessness, guilt, anxiety, or depression.
6. "Chasing" losses—in other words, after losing money gambling, coming back soon afterward with the aim of getting even.
7. Lying to family members, a therapist, or others to conceal the extent of involvement with gambling.
8. Committing illegal acts such as forgery, fraud, theft, or embezzlement to finance gambling.
9. Having jeopardized or lost a significant relationship, job, or educational or career opportunity because of gambling.
10. Relying on others to provide money to relieve a desperate financial situation caused by gambling.

A person who exhibits fewer than five of the diagnostic criteria may be a *problem gambler*. In 1997, the Harvard Medical School Division on Addictions, using "past year" measures, estimated that 2.2 million adults in the United States were pathological gamblers and 5.3 million were problem gamblers.

The APA distinguishes pathological gambling from *social gambling*, which typically occurs with friends and lasts for a limited period of time with predetermined acceptable losses; and *professional gambling*, in which the gambler limits his or her risks and discipline is central to betting. Neither social gambling nor professional gambling is considered a disorder.

*Source: American Psychiatric Association, *Diagnostic and Statistical Manual of Mental Disorders*. 4th ed. (Washington, DC: American Psychiatric Association, 1994).

Legalized gambling invites corruption.

A casino license is a valuable business asset because, in most states, only a limited few are issued. Public officials have wide discretion in granting licenses, and that carries the potential for corruption. That happened in Louisiana, where former Governor Edwin Edwards was charged with extorting some $3 million:

Edwards and his longtime political lieutenants have intervened in the decisions of public agencies that are supposed to be independent, influencing everything from small-time video poker license applications to the 15 cherished riverboat licenses, worth potentially millions of dollars to the holders, and millions more to some of the people they hired.[23] Edwards was found guilty of a variety of federal crimes, and went to prison in 2001.

Like other industries, the gaming industry uses its wealth to influence federal and state gambling policy. According to the Center for Responsive Politics, the industry contributed nearly $11.8 million to congressional candidates from 2005 to 2006. The industry also hires former government officials as lobbyists, people who meet with lawmakers and their staff and make the case for legislation favorable to a particular industry. In Illinois, for example, casino companies made an all-out effort to expand legalized gambling. Robert Goodman observed, "this situation took on almost farcical proportions—at one time, former Governor Jim Thompson, former Senate President Philip Rock, former House Majority Leader James McPike, and former Chicago Mayor Eugene Sawyer were all registered lobbyists for the casino industry."[24]

Corruption has also occurred in connection with Indian gaming, which is regulated at the federal level. "For cautionary tales," says writer Richard Hoffer, "Indians have the example of the Tigua tribe, whose rollicking Speaking Rock Casino was all but shuttered when Texas won a federal lawsuit against them. A 1500-slot outfit, with revenues of $60 million a year, is now nearly defunct. Gone are the $15,000 a year members received from casino profits."[25] The Tigua, it turned out, were the victims of Jack Abramoff, a powerful lobbyist with ties to congressional leaders. In 2006, Abramoff went to prison after pleading guilty to a number of federal charges, which included defrauding Indian tribes of millions of dollars. After he and his colleagues played a role in closing Speaking Rock, Abramoff told the Tigua that he could persuade Congress to reopen it. The tribe paid $4.2 million in lobbying fees, but the casino never reopened.

Additionally, some believe that the casino industry is not totally free of organized crime. In 1990, the Chicago Crime Commission warned city officials, who were considering a downtown casino, that "organized crime will infiltrate casino operations and unions, and will be involved in related loan-sharking, prostitution, drug activities . . . and public corruption."[26]

Gambling undermines the work ethic.

Church leaders have long argued that gambling subverts people's work ethic by making them greedy and by offering financial gain for nothing. Gambling critic Robert Goodman also contends that gambling has helped make the United States a "culture of chance" in which people think they can get rich by speculating in stocks, real estate, and even baseball cards. He argues that such a culture demeans work:

We handsomely reward the designers of clever lottery scratch tickets and analysts who chart the future value of collectible trinkets, while we neglect the talents that built our basic industries. What we are creating is a scavenger economy that relies more on the milking of existing wealth than on the creation of new wealth. It is quite possible that at no other time in history have so many people been trying so hard to make money without having to work for it.[27]

Paul Simon, an opponent of legalized gambling, contended that gambling adds nothing of value to the economy. During a Senate debate, he said:

Gambling Terms

Banking game: A game in which players risk their money against the casino's money. Most popular casino games, such as blackjack and craps, are banking games.

Book, Bookmaker: A book is an establishment or a special area of a casino that takes wagers on horse races and sporting events. A bookmaker, or "bookie," is a person who collects and pays off the bets. Bookmaking is legal only in Nevada.

Casino win: The amount that the casino retains after paying out winners, also referred to as *gross gaming revenue*

Expected win rate: A percentage of the total amount of money wagered that a bettor can expect to win back. For example, a player who bets a given number at a roulette table has an expected win rate of about 95 percent. If that person makes 100 consecutive one-dollar bets on that number, he or she can expect to end the night with $95.

Gaming: The word originally used to describe *gambling*, and the term preferred by the casino industry

Handle: The sum of all money wagered. Most of the handle is paid back to bettors, leaving the casino with a small percentage.

House advantage: The mathematical edge a casino provides for itself by paying winning gamblers at less than the true odds. The house advantage varies depending on the type of bet that is made. It is also known as the "house edge" or "edge."

Instant lottery ticket: A lottery ticket that contains a number of hidden symbols. A bettor who "scratches off" (removes the covering from) a particular combination of symbols wins a prize.

Jackpot: The top prize awarded by a lottery for matching all of the numbers drawn. If no ticket matches all the numbers, the jackpot "rolls over" to the next drawing and increases in size.

Keno: A game in which a set of numbers (typically 20) is drawn from a large field of numbers (typically 80). Players select a smaller set of numbers, and winners are awarded prizes based on how many of their numbers match those in the drawn set. This is traditionally a casino game, but some state lotteries offer keno games in establishments such as bars.

Lotto: A lottery game in which players select a group of numbers from a large set and are awarded prizes based on how many of their numbers match those drawn by lottery officials. The amount of the prize depends on how many drawn numbers the player matched. Powerball and Mega Millions are multistate lotto games. The largest lotto jackpot in U.S. history was $365 million.

Marker: A check that can be written at the gaming tables by a player who has established credit with the casino. Players can also bet with borrowed money by taking a cash advance on their credit cards.

Non-banking game: A game in which players bet against one another instead of the casino. Poker is the most popular non-banking game.

Odds: The ratio at which a winning bet will be paid. For example, 3-to-1 odds means that for every $1 wagered, the bettor will receive $3 in winnings.

Off-track betting (OTB): Pari-mutuel wagering conducted on a race at a location other than the racetrack where the race is actually being run

Pari-mutuel wagering: A system of wagering that is used in horse racing. All wagers are placed in a pool, and the winners' payoff depends on the total number of winning wagers. Not all of the money in the pool is paid back to winners. The racetrack sets aside a commission, known as the *takeout*, which is used to pay taxes, expenses, and prizes to owners of winning horses.

Payout: The amount of money paid back to winning gamblers

Payout percentage: The percent of each dollar wagered that is returned to winning bettors. In the case of slot and video poker machines, the payout percentage varies by machine, but is typically in the range of 90 percent.

Probability: A branch of mathematics that measures the likelihood that an event will occur. Probabilities are expressed as numbers between 0 and 1. The probability of an impossible event is 0, while an event that is certain to occur has a probability of 1.

Progressive jackpot: A term used to refer to a jackpot that continues to grow until someone wins it; often used in connection with slot machines

(continues)

(continued)

Rake: A percentage of the total amount bet that is set aside and paid to the casino. The rake is used in non-banking games such as poker, where players do not bet against the casino but rather against one another.

Simulcast wagering: Pari-mutuel wagering on a horse race that is run at a track other than the location where the wagers are placed

True odds: The actual chance of winning. For example, a roulette wheel has 38 numbers: 1 through 36, and single zero (0) and double zero (00). The true odds that a given number will come up are 37 to 1. Because a casino must earn a profit to stay in business, it pays winners at less than true odds. Thus the usual payout on a winning number in roulette is 35 to 1.

Video Lottery Terminal (VLT): An electronic game of chance that is played on a video screen. VLTs often simulate popular casino games such as blackjack, poker, and slot machines.

The distinguished Nobel Prize–winning economist Paul Samuelson has warned us: "There is a substantial economic case to be made against gambling. It involves simply sterile transfers of money or goods between individuals, creating no new money or goods. Although it creates no output, gambling does nevertheless absorb time and resources. When pursued beyond the limits of recreation . . . gambling subtracts from the national income.[28]

Furthermore, the gambling industry does not develop products such as new medicines or advanced technology that will expand the economy and improve people's quality of life.

Summary

The spread of legalized gambling has been harmful to society in a number of ways. To begin with, it has led to a substantial increase in pathological gambling, especially among young people. People who cannot control their gambling often find themselves in serious financial trouble. Some steal money to keep playing, and others go bankrupt. Gambling has also been linked to domestic problems, suicide, and corruption of public officials, and communities that allow it experience higher crime rates. Finally, gambling adds nothing of value to the economy, contributing to a "culture of chance" that rewards luck rather than hard work.

Gambling Prohibition Does More Harm Than Good

In their book *The Business of Risk*, Vicki Abt and her co-authors observed that "gambling is a universal cultural phenomenon: one of a relatively small number of activities that occur in nearly all societies and every period. People have been playing risky games for at least 4,000 years, and virtually every culture has evolved ways of letting its members stake something of value on an event of uncertain outcome."[29] In spite of gaming's popularity, many societies, including the United States, have tried to outlaw it. As a result, "the history of gambling in America is the history of a contradiction: From colonial times, Americans have bet on horses and bought lottery tickets, all the while condemning gambling as vice."[30] Many people believe that past laws against gambling led to even worse consequences than gaming itself.

Critics exaggerate gaming's harmful effects.

The case for prohibiting gaming rests in large part on the perception that legalizing it has led to serious social consequences, such as a substantial increase in pathological gambling. Those consequences are not, however, as serious as claimed. The Public Sector Gaming Study Commission, an organization of state legislators who sit on committees that regulate gaming, reported in 2000:

> In short, there is no solid basis for concluding that the wider legalization of gambling, which has cut into illegal gambling and friendly betting, has caused a concomitant increase in pathological gambling. In fact, it appears that pathological gambling is quite rare within the general population [and] it does not appear to be increasing in frequency.[31]

In 1975, the Commission on the Review of the National Policy Toward Gambling estimated that less than 1 percent of people in the United States were "probable compulsive" gamblers. Twenty-four years later, the National Research Council estimated that 0.9 percent of American adults were pathological gamblers during the past year and 1.5 percent were pathological gamblers at some point in their lives. A study published in the *Journal of Clinical Psychiatry* in 2005 produced an even more modest estimate: Compulsive gamblers made up only 0.42 percent of the population.

Another often-heard argument is that legalized gaming breeds crime. The Public Sector Gaming Study Commission also discounted this:

> The majority of the information collected during the past decade indicates there is no link between gambling, particularly casino-style gambling, and crime. The security on the premises of gambling facilities, the multiple layers of

FROM THE BENCH

Does the Wire Act Apply to Online Gambling?
United States v. Cohen

It is believed that the first casino went online and began taking bets in 1995. Since then, hundreds of gambling businesses have established an online presence. They typically offer casino gaming, sports betting, and interactive poker games. Because Congress has not passed a law that directly regulates online gaming, federal officials continue to rely on the Interstate Wire Act of 1961 to pursue the operators of gambling Web sites.

The controversy over online gambling deepened after a number of other countries (25 countries as of 1999) legalized it. Most online gambling Web sites are based in the Caribbean and Central America. Even though online casinos could not legally operate in the United States, they nevertheless targeted the vast American market. Many casinos offered sports betting, which is illegal in the United States except for in-person bets at licensed Nevada sports books.

Because online casinos are located outside the United States, the Wire Act raises the legal issue of *jurisdiction*—that is, whether the U.S. government has the authority to regulate transactions between Americans and foreign Web sites. As the National Gambling Impact Study Commission observed:

> Where are bets and wagers taking place on the Internet? Are they taking place at the site where the person downloads a Web page onto a personal computer? Is the bet taking place at the point of financial transactions—that is, where the bank account, credit card, or smart card companies are located? Or is the bet or wager occurring at the ISP [Internet service provider] that hosts the Internet gambling site?*

During the late 1990s, a federal crackdown on offshore sports bookmakers led to a legal challenge as to whether the Wire Act applied. As the result of an FBI investigation, a grand jury charged 22 people with Wire Act violations. Fifteen pled guilty to various charges, and six remained outside the United States and became fugitives.

The only defendant who came home and fought the charges was Jay Cohen. He and his partners had established the World Sports Exchange (WSE), which took bets on professional and college sports. WSE operated on the Caribbean island of Antigua, whose government had legalized online casinos, but the business advertised on a variety of media that reached would-be bettors in the United States. Cohen and his partners took the position that Antigua-based casinos were outside the Wire Act's jurisdiction. The U.S. government, however, argued that the act applied to WSE because Cohen and his partners advertised to Americans and encouraged them to open accounts.

After the trial, a federal court jury found Cohen guilty of all charges, and the judge sentenced him to 21 months in prison and fined him $5,000. Cohen appealed to the U.S. Court of Appeals for the Second Circuit, which, in *United States v. Cohen*, affirmed the judgment. Judge John Keenan wrote the court's opinion.

Judge Keenan first rejected Cohen's contention that the Wire Act did not apply because sports betting was illegal in neither New York State nor Antigua. He cited language in New York's state constitution that expressly prohibited bookmaking and also prohibited any other form of gambling other than the lottery and pari-mutuel wagering at racetracks or government-run off-track betting facilities. Judge Keenan also concluded that WSE had "transmitted" bets within the meaning of the Wire Act because so long as a bettor had an account that was in good standing, WSE personnel accepted his or her bets, no questions asked. Finally, Judge Keenan found it irrelevant for the purposes of the Wire Act that a bettor had to establish an account before betting, stating that account wagering was wagering nonetheless.

Even though the courts have held that the Wire Act can be applied to offshore Web sites, several problems remain. To begin with, the Wire Act appears to outlaw only sports betting and not casinos or poker. (Some experts believe that the law could be used against other forms of gambling as well.) The United States cannot directly enforce its gambling laws against businesses that are operating legally in other countries, or arrest individual violators unless they are found inside the United States. It is also more difficult to shut down a Web site than it is to close a "bricks-and-mortar" business, because the Web site's owners can simply move it to another Internet address. Finally, gambling Web sites cannot survive unless there is a demand for them, and federal law does not bar Americans from placing a bet online.

* National Gambling Impact and Policy Commission, *The National Gambling Impact Study Commission: final report* (Washington, DC: The Commission, 1999), 5–7.

regulatory control, and the economic and social benefits that gambling seem to offer to communities are effective deterrents of criminal activity.[32]

Atlantic City, in particular, has been portrayed as crime-ridden. Shortly after the introduction of casinos in 1978, the crime rate in Atlantic City seemingly spiked, but after that the situation improved. Between 1988 and 2001, the crime rate in Atlantic City dropped every year except one. If crime figures are adjusted to reflect the millions of people who visit, Atlantic City's crime rate has in fact fallen by nearly 50 percent from where it was before casinos opened.

It is also debatable whether other supposed consequences of legalized gaming are as serious as alleged. Gaming has been linked to an increase in bankruptcies, but a 1999 U.S. Department of the Treasury study found no connection between the availability of gaming and bankruptcy rates. In fact, the two states with the highest bankruptcy rates in 2002 were Utah, which has no legalized gaming at all, and Tennessee, which in 2002 had neither casino gaming nor a state lottery. Casinos in particular have been charged with exploiting older Americans, but a 2003 study funded by the National Institute of Justice found no support for that accusation; in fact, the study found that older players gambled more responsibly than Americans as a whole.

Finally, casinos have been accused of "cannibalizing" customers from existing businesses. Researchers at the University of New Orleans found the opposite, that the opening of casinos increased the number of local food and beverage establishments and the number of people who worked in them.

Prohibition merely drives gambling underground.

Gaming prohibition has always proved unenforceable. David Schwartz, the director of the Center for Gaming Studies at the University of Nevada, Las Vegas, observed, "In 1646, Massachusetts passed a law that banned gambling in public houses—the first such law in the colonies—but enforcement was lax, with few church members actually fined for gambling."[33] Today, as well, the enforcement of gaming laws is spotty. In 2004, the nation's law enforcement authorities made only 10,755 gambling-related arrests, compared to nearly 14 million arrests for all offenses.

Vicki Abt and colleagues contend: "Prohibition was the original sin. It removed gambling from the realm of legitimate economic endeavor but failed to eliminate, or even to measurably decrease, the American propensity to gamble. The inevitable result was the creation of vast markets for commercial gambling which had no legal supplier."[34] In other words, prohibition drives gaming underground—and often into the hands of organized crime. During the nineteenth century, "gambling syndicates" got around the law by making business deals with local authorities. In New York City, for instance, thousands of gaming houses operated illegally. David Schwartz explains the arrangement:

> Professional gamblers, gangs, and politicians of this era shared a growing affinity that ultimately led to the creation of gambling syndicates. Gambling house operators needed protection from both the law and the lawless: Zealous police could enforce antigambling ordinances and judges might impose harsh penalties for running a gambling house, while gangs of rowdies might terrorize the house and its patrons. Thus, professional gamblers reached out to the law with graft and employed the outlaws as bouncers.[35]

As a result, gaming syndicates had monopoly power, the government took in no tax revenue, and victims of cheating had no legal recourse.

Sports betting provides a modern-day example of why prohibition does not work. Even though many forms of gaming are widely available, betting on sports is legal only in Nevada sports books. Nevertheless, the National Gambling Impact Study Commission (NGISC) called sports betting the most widespread and popular form of gaming in America, with an estimated $80 billion to $380 billion wagered every year. Only a tiny percentage of that amount—$2.43 billion in 2006—is wagered legally. There is reason to believe that the underworld handles much of the illegal betting on sports. According to a 2007 status report on gambling, "As the casinos were taken over by corporations, organized

Card Counting: Beating Casinos at Blackjack

In most casino games, the outcome is decided strictly by chance: One spin of the wheel or throw of the dice has no effect on the next one. That is not true of blackjack, which became popular in Las Vegas during the 1960s. Kevin Lewis, who reportedly won more than a million dollars playing blackjack, explains:

Blackjack is the only game in the casino that is beatable over an extended period of time, because blackjack is subject to *continuous probability*. This simply means that what you see affects what you are going to see. Blackjack is a game with a memory. If an ace comes out in the first round of a blackjack shoe, that means there is one *less* ace left in the rest of the deck. The odds of drawing another ace have gone down by a calculable fraction. In other words, the past has an effect on the future.*

It is therefore possible for a blackjack player to mentally count the cards that have been played and recognize situations where the odds favor the player, not the casino. Some players, like Lewis, were so skillful at counting cards that they could win at blackjack on a regular basis.

Lewis belonged to a card-counting team based at the Massachusetts Institute of Technology. The MIT card counters succeeded for a while but were eventually caught by casino security and banned from playing. "They couldn't arrest you, but in Las Vegas, they could kick you out of the casino," Lewis said. Section 463.0129(3)(a) of the Nevada Revised Statutes affirms the "common-law right of a gaming establishment to exclude any person from gaming activities or eject any person from the premises of the establishment for any reason." Nevada's courts have ruled that casinos may exclude or eject players for card counting, or even just for winning. A. William Maupin, a justice of the Supreme Court of Nevada, summed up the legal status of card counting:

crime strengthened its hold on illegal bookmaking. Although law enforcement officials acknowledge that many 'independent' bookies operate throughout the country, the big money in illegal sports gambling is still controlled by organized crime."[36]

Justin Wolfers, a professor at the Wharton School at the University of Pennsylvania, argues that prohibition makes betting

---

On one hand, gaming establishments have the unquestioned right to protect themselves against so-called "card counters" who have developed expertise in the game of "blackjack" ("twenty-one"). On the other hand, neither card counting nor the use of a legal subterfuge such as a disguise to gain access to this table game is illegal under Nevada law.**

In the early days of legalized gambling in Atlantic City, Ken Uston, one of the most famous card counters of all time, argued that casinos had no legal right to eject him. In *Uston v. Resorts International Hotel, Inc.*, the Supreme Court of New Jersey agreed with him. The justices reasoned that the state's gaming laws spelled out the rules of blackjack so completely that casinos did not have the authority to impose new rules aimed at card counters.

The *Uston* decision did not end the controversy. In 1989 the New Jersey Casino Control Commission authorized casinos to take "countermeasures" against card counters, including ordering a reshuffle or changing the maximum bet limit at any time. In a lawsuit brought by a card counter who argued that he had been discriminated against, Judge Nicea D'Annunzio of the Superior Court's Appellate Division concluded that the commission allowed casinos to treat card counters differently than other players: "The Commission adopted these measures to hobble card counters because of their perceived threat to the mathematical advantage the casino industry must enjoy to remain vital."***

* Ben Mezrich, *Bringing Down the House: The Inside Story of Six M.I.T Students Who Took Vegas for Millions* (New York: The Free Press, 2002), 252–253.

** *Chen v. State Gaming Control Board*, 994 P.2d 1151, 1153 (Nev. Sup. Ct. 2000) (Maupin, J., dissenting).

*** *Campione v. Adamar of New Jersey*, 302 N.J. Super. 99, 110, 694 A.2d 1045, 1050 (App. Div. 1997).

scandals *more* likely because it occurs either in the unregulated underworld or in barely regulated foreign countries that allow online casinos to operate. Wolfers and others point out that over the years, legal bookmakers have tipped off the authorities to possible fixed games. In order to make a profit, a sports bookmaker must set the betting line where equal amounts are wagered on each side. Tamara Audi and Adam Thompson, reporters at *The Wall Street Journal*, explain why bookmakers want game fixers brought to justice:

> When bets come in disproportionately, casinos move the betting line in an attempt to re-equalize wagers on each side. But if a gambler succeeds in placing a large bet on one side and then illicitly assures the outcome, casinos lose money unfairly.
>
> Las Vegas bookies say this gives them a motivation to police against match fixing. They also say their reams of performance and betting-flow data can be used to flag unusual patterns.[37]

Gambling prohibition is archaic and hypocritical.

David Schwartz explains that the Puritans' dislike of gaming was rooted in their work ethic: "Godly men and women should, instead of chatting over cards, be preparing themselves to enter heaven's kingdom."[38] Schwartz also points out that the Puritans did in fact play cards, an early reflection of the hypocrisy of those who favor prohibition.

The enforcement of gambling laws has been marked by a double standard: Authorities often winked at betting by the rich but cracked down on betting by working people. In colonial society, it was not only acceptable but also *expected* for wealthy men to bet on horse races and even cockfights and dogfights. During the nineteenth century authorities in some cities, such as New Orleans, tolerated high-end casinos even though they were officially illegal. Even smaller towns had "clubs" started by local "sporting gentlemen." These were clandestine meeting places where men drank (often in defiance of Prohibition laws), smoked cigars, and gambled.

The double standard has continued to this day. During the stock market "bubble" of 1999 to 2000, many Americans bought shares of stock of companies they knew nothing about because they expected the price of those shares to rise indefinitely. Some bought shares with borrowed money. Others engaged in "day trading," buying shares in hopes of making a quick profit, sometimes within minutes. Some day traders who guessed wrong lost their life's savings, and a few became so distraught that they killed themselves or others. Jackson Lears, a professor at Rutgers University, insists that there is little difference between market speculation and gaming:

> Stock trading may breed pathological or destructive behavior, but it is seldom subjected to the clinical gaze of psychiatry—and even more rarely, in recent years, to the baleful stare of moralists. Even now, when we know that much of the bull market prosperity was based on fraud, moral outrage tends to focus on the confidence men who rigged the game rather than the game itself. As official thought leaders squirm to protect investor confidence, stock trading preserves a precarious legitimacy. Gambling, in contrast, remains a perfect target for dissection, disapproval, and oversimplification.[39]

Some of the worst hypocrisy surrounds sports betting. The NCAA, which regulates college sports, favors a nationwide ban on betting on amateur sports. Richard Hoffer argues, "Where does the NCAA think its dough is coming from? Try to remember: CBS paid the NCAA $6 billion for the right to televise the tournament for 11 years. Nobody thinks the games are *that* good."[40] Hoffer's argument can be made about professional sports, too.

The nation's news media also have been accused of hypocrisy toward sports betting. The sports sections of many local newspapers publish the betting lines on upcoming games, and some publications run advertisements from "touts" who claim to have inside information for bettors.

FROM THE BENCH

Is Poker a Game of Skill?
Joker Club v. Hardin

After Congress passed the Unlawful Internet Gaming Enforcement Act of 2006 (UIGEA), organizations such as the Poker Players Alliance argued that UIGEA should be amended to exempt poker, which they insist is a game of skill. Others had made this argument in the past, and a number of states recognize a distinction between games of chance and games of skill. California, for example, allows "card rooms" to operate. A card room is a location where people can play poker and sometimes other card games for money. Unlike a casino, a card room does not compete against the players. Instead, it takes a percentage of the amount bet.

In recent years, poker has again become popular in the United States. A business called The Joker Club, LLC, wanted to capitalize on this trend by opening a poker club in Durham County, North Carolina. It asked the local district attorney whether such a business would be legal under §14–292 of the General Statutes of North Carolina, which provided that "any person ... that operates any game of chance ... at which any money, property, or other thing of value is bet ... shall be guilty of a Class 2 misdemeanor."

The district attorney concluded that poker was a game of chance and therefore illegal. The Joker Club filed a lawsuit in the Superior Court, challenging this interpretation of the law. At the trial, experts for the club argued that poker was primarily a game of skill. Even though chance might allow a skilled player to lose a single hand of poker, he or she would eventually prevail over less-skilled players. The experts explained that skilled players were more experienced, more disciplined, better able to remember what cards have been dealt and how that affects the odds, and better able to "read" opposing players. An expert witness for

Gaming prohibition offends American notions of liberty.

Gaming prohibition raises the question of whether the government has any business punishing people for behavior that does not directly harm others. Many Americans believe that prosecuting "victimless crimes" has no place in a free society. In recent years, laws against some such victimless crimes, especially those

FROM THE BENCH

the state testified that luck prevailed over skill. He cited as an example a televised poker tournament in which a hand with a 91 percent chance of winning lost to a hand with only a 9 percent chance of winning.

The Superior Court agreed with the district attorney and concluded that poker was a game of chance. The Joker Club appealed to the Court of Appeals, which affirmed that decision. Judge Ann Marie Calabria wrote the appeals court's opinion. She first observed that a game that could be determined by superior skill was not a game of chance. "For example, bowling, chess, and billiards are games of skill because skill determines the outcome. The game itself is static and the only factor separating the players is their relative skill levels." Poker, however, was different. She wrote: "Although skills such as knowledge of human psychology, bluffing, and the ability to calculate and analyze odds make it more likely for skilled players to defeat novices, novices may yet prevail with a simple run of luck. No amount of skill can change a deuce into an ace."

The Joker Club contended that poker was analogous to golf. It argued that a weekend golfer might beat Tiger Woods on a single hole, but had virtually no chance of beating him in an 18-hole round. Judge Calabria rejected that analogy, explaining:

In golf, as in bowling or billiards, the players are presented with an equal challenge, with each determining his fortune by his own skill. Although chance inevitably intervenes, it is not inherent in the game and does not overcome skill, and the player maintains the opportunity to defeat chance with superior skill. Whereas in poker, a skilled player may give himself a statistical advantage but is always subject to defeat at the turn of a card, an instrumentality beyond his control.

The Joker Club appealed the decision to the Supreme Court of North Carolina, which as of the publication of this book has not yet handed down a ruling.

involving consensual sexual behavior, have either been repealed or found unconstitutional. Vicki Abt and colleagues see these laws as undemocratic:

If the solution to abuse by a minority—of activities or substances or even freedoms—is prohibition for everyone, *anything* can become "wrong," and society is faced with a kind of tyranny. It is a basic tenet of democracy that in a free society people live the way they want to live, not the way some reformers, however well-intentioned, think they should.[41]

In the case of gambling, the minority in question is small indeed. Studies compiled for the NGISC indicate that 94 percent of Americans who gamble do so without ever getting into trouble. In fact, the number of compulsive gamblers in the United States is considerably smaller than the number of people who have drinking problems, even though alcohol is legal in all 50 states.

The National Research Council found that more than 80 percent of American adults said that they had placed a bet at some point in their lives. As a result, prohibitionists must resort to fear to make their case. "Since the targeted behavior is usually highly popular and widespread, prohibitionists must redefine it as an unconditional evil that cannot be resisted, even by men and women of character," explains Nick Gillespie, who is now the editor in chief of the libertarian magazine *Reason*. "Ironically, in the name of morality, prohibitionists must strip individuals of the right to make moral decisions."[42]

Gaming prohibitionists have often portrayed gamers as deviants. Jackson Lears explains why: "The image of the devil as a gambler captured the moral stakes in the war on gambling (at least from the warrior's point of view). This was not simply an attempt to reform individual conduct, as the war on alcohol claimed to be; this was an attempt to abolish an alternative culture."[43] This reflects the lingering belief among some that gaming, like drinking alcohol or having sex outside marriage, is sinful and therefore must be outlawed. However sincere those beliefs are, Vicki Abt and her colleagues counter that "meaningful policies and effective laws and regulation cannot be created from the assumption that gambling is a sin and inherently evil."[44] Charles Murray, a fellow at the American Enterprise Institute, further argued:

> Society is weakened every time a law is passed that large numbers of reasonable, responsible citizens think is stupid. Such laws invite good citizens to choose knowingly to break the law, confident that they are doing nothing morally wrong. . . .
>
> The temptation for good citizens to ignore a stupid law is encouraged when it is unenforceable. In this, the attempt to ban Internet gambling is exemplary.[45]

Murray's comments were directed at the Unlawful Internet Gambling Enforcement Act of 2006 (UIGEA). Murray and others see laws such as UIGEA as a form of paternalism: Government is attempting to protect adults from the consequences of spending their own money in the privacy of their own homes. Gamers insist that no such protection is needed.

Summary

Opponents have exaggerated the negative consequences of legalized gaming, especially the link between legalization and the extent of pathological gambling. History makes it clear that prohibition never eliminated gaming, but merely drove it underground, where it fell into the hands of the underworld and led to the corruption of public officials. Gaming prohibition is a remnant of religious teaching that gaming is sinful and those who participate in it are deviants. Since colonial times, gaming laws have been unevenly enforced, and the brunt of enforcement has often fallen on poorer Americans. Laws against gaming are contrary to many people's beliefs that government has no business prohibiting behavior that does not harm third parties.

Legalized Gambling Has Adverse Economic and Political Consequences

During the 1980s, Lee Iacocca was one of the most admired corporate executives in the United States. He took charge of Chrysler Corporation when it faced bankruptcy, and persuaded the federal government to lend it more than $1 billion to stay alive. Iacocca's leadership saved Chrysler and saved thousands of jobs.

There is, however, another chapter in Iacocca's biography, which author Robert Goodman reveals:

> Only 10 years after his feat at Chrysler, Iacocca had switched gears. By 1994, he had left the company, moved to Los Angeles, and set up his own investment company. The new focus of his business was gambling, including efforts to open casinos in Michigan's economically depressed cities and futuristic concepts such as in-flight gambling for airline passengers.[46]

Opponents of legalized gambling contend that when businessmen like Iacocca conclude that it is easier to make money building casinos than it is to build cars, gambling has distorted the economic and social priorities in the United States.

The gambling industry profits at the expense of communities.

The gambling industry generates what economists call "externalities"—that is, the negative impact of economic activity on the rest of society. Robert Goodman explains that, "in much the same way that a company which pollutes the environment and doesn't have to pay for the cleanup costs can show handsome profits, a casino that cannibalizes a local economy and produces increased problem-gambling behavior can also show its stockholders enormous returns on investment."[47]

Casinos generate a great deal of wealth for their shareholders and executives, in part because they can push the social costs of compulsive gambling onto others. For example, employers pay for gambling-related absenteeism and white-collar crime, while states and cities pay for law enforcement and treatment. Nevada is the worst offender because it reaps the benefits of gambling by millions of visitors, and then "exports" the costs of that gambling to the visitors' home states.

Compulsive gambling is not the only externality. Casinos put a strain on the infrastructure of nearby communities. William Hasse, the planning director for a small town in Connecticut, told the National Gambling Impact Study Commission (NGISC) about the impact of Foxwoods, a huge tribal casino in the area:

> The three local host communities . . . with a combined population of only 25,300, find it difficult to cope with the magnitude of Foxwoods Casino, primarily in the areas of diminished quality of life due to tremendous increases in traffic along local roads and state highways, deteriorating highway infrastructure, and increased policing and emergency

services costs. . . . Foxwoods has expanded so rapidly that the host towns and Connecticut Department of Transportation have been unable to keep up.[48]

Casinos also generate building sprawl and pollution. In some communities, they trigger land speculation, which results in long-time residents being forced out of their homes to make room for gambling-related construction.

Where Gambling Is Legal

Every state except Hawaii and Utah has some form of legalized gambling, but state laws vary widely as to what forms of gambling are allowed. The following is a list of those states that offer popular forms of gambling.

Commercial casinos are legal in 12 states: Colorado, Illinois, Indiana, Iowa, Louisiana, Michigan, Mississippi, Missouri, Nevada, New Jersey, Pennsylvania, and South Dakota.

Indian gaming facilities operate in 28 states: Alabama, Alaska, Arizona, California, Colorado, Connecticut, Florida, Idaho, Iowa, Kansas, Louisiana, Michigan, Minnesota, Mississippi, Missouri, Montana, Nebraska, New Mexico, New York, North Carolina, North Dakota, Oklahoma, Oregon, South Dakota, Texas, Washington, Wisconsin, and Wyoming. Tribes in Alabama, Alaska, and Wyoming offer bingo only and no casino-type games.

A total of 41 states, plus the District of Columbia, offer lotteries: Arizona, California, Colorado, Connecticut, Delaware, District of Columbia, Florida, Georgia, Idaho, Illinois, Indiana, Iowa, Kansas, Kentucky, Louisiana, Maine, Maryland, Massachusetts, Michigan, Minnesota, Missouri, Montana, Nebraska, New Hampshire, New Jersey, New Mexico, New York, North Carolina, Ohio, Oklahoma, Oregon, Pennsylvania, Rhode Island, South Carolina, South Dakota, Tennessee, Texas, Vermont, Virginia, Washington, West Virginia, and Wisconsin.

A total of 43 states permit pari-mutuel wagering: Alabama, Arizona, Arkansas, California, Colorado, Connecticut, Delaware, Florida, Idaho, Illinois, Indiana, Iowa, Kansas, Kentucky, Louisiana, Maine, Maryland, Massachusetts, Michigan,

Legalized gambling does not benefit local economies.

Casinos revived Nevada's economy, but gambling opponents insist that the state is unique. Robert Goodman explains: "Nevada has a relatively small budget to support with gambling revenues. Although Nevada has no lottery, taxes on gambling in 1994 constituted about 40 percent of the state budget. By the early 1980s it was already estimated that roughly one-half of

Minnesota, Missouri, Montana, Nebraska, Nevada, New Hampshire, New Jersey, New Mexico, New York, North Dakota, Ohio, Oklahoma, Oregon, Pennsylvania, Rhode Island, South Dakota, Tennessee, Texas, Vermont, Virginia, Washington, West Virginia, Wisconsin, and Wyoming. (Even though pari-mutuel wagering is legal in Tennessee, no racetracks were operating as of 2008.)

There are 11 states that permit racetrack casinos, or "racinos": Delaware, Florida, Iowa, Louisiana, Maine, New Mexico, New York, Oklahoma, Pennsylvania, Rhode Island, and West Virginia.

Video lottery terminals are legal in 8 states: Delaware, Louisiana, Montana, New York, Oregon, Rhode Island, South Dakota, and West Virginia.

A total of 47 states, plus the District of Columbia, permit some form of charitable gambling: Alabama, Alaska, Arizona, Arkansas, California, Colorado, Connecticut, Delaware, District of Columbia, Florida, Georgia, Idaho, Illinois, Indiana, Iowa, Kansas, Kentucky, Louisiana, Maine, Maryland, Massachusetts, Michigan, Minnesota, Mississippi, Missouri, Montana, Nebraska, Nevada, New Hampshire, New Jersey, New Mexico, New York, North Carolina, North Dakota, Ohio, Oklahoma, Oregon, Pennsylvania, Rhode Island, South Carolina, South Dakota, Texas, Vermont, Virginia, Washington, West Virginia, Wisconsin, and Wyoming.

Sources:

American Gaming Association, *Fact Sheets on Gaming Industry Issues* (Washington, DC: American Gaming Association, 2003).

John W. Weier, ed., *Gambling: What's at Stake?* (Detroit: Thomson Gale, 2007).

Joe Rodgers, chairman of the Gambling Free Tennessee Alliance, speaks at a news conference in Nashville in 2002. Lottery opponents took part in a statewide protest to dispute supporters' claims that a lottery would help the state's economy.

all jobs in Nevada were either directly or indirectly dependent on the gambling industry."[49] Because Nevada is comparatively remote, visitors tend to stay for multiple days and spend on food, lodging, and entertainment as well as gambling. That money cycles through the state's economy, generating economic activity and creating jobs.

Atlantic City, however, has not enjoyed the same success. Goodman described what happened instead:

> Despite some $6 billion of private investment in casino-related facilities, the promised economic renaissance never happened. Atlantic City became virtually two cities—one of extravagant casinos, largely manned by an outside work force,

and the other, a city of boarded-up buildings and a predominantly minority population that suffered massive unemployment and was given easy access to gambling. . . .

As Atlantic City became a center for casino gambling and ceased to be a beach resort, the remaining hotels and businesses that once catered to tourists and the local population were increasingly left without even the remnants of their former customer base.[50]

One witness told the NGISC that in 1978, the year the first casino opened, there were 311 taverns and restaurants in Atlantic City. Nineteen years later, only 66 remained. The witness also said that many of the local businesses that remained were pawnshops, cash-for-gold stores, and discount outlets.

Much the same thing happened in Deadwood, South Dakota, when casinos arrived. Jeffrey Bloomberg, the local prosecuting attorney, told a U.S. House committee:

[The people of Deadwood] were promised "economic development, new jobs, and lower taxes." Instead, casinos flourished, but other businesses did not. Businesses that provide the necessities of life such as clothing are no longer available . . . and customers of the town's only remaining grocery store walk a gauntlet of slot-machines as they exit with their purchases.[51]

Bloomberg added that taxes on both residential and commercial property rose every year since gambling was legalized in Deadwood.

Legalized gambling also makes a community an unattractive place to live and work. Gambling opponent John Warren Kindt, a professor at the University of Illinois, argues that most companies do not want to absorb the social costs that result from legalized gambling. In addition, many would-be workers do not want to raise a family in a community with widespread gambling. Jan

The Indian Gaming Regulatory Act

The Supreme Court's decision in *California v. Cabazon Band of Mission Indians* swept aside many state laws that restricted Native American gaming, and created regulatory uncertainty. Congress addressed that problem the following year by passing the Indian Gaming Regulatory Act of 1988.

Congress found that numerous tribes had entered the gaming business; federal law did not provide clear regulations for tribal gaming; and federal policy was to promote economic development, self-sufficiency, and strong tribal government. Congress summed up the law governing tribal gaming: "Indian tribes have the exclusive right to regulate gaming activity on Indian lands if the gaming activity is not specifically prohibited by federal law and is conducted within a State which does not, as a matter of criminal law and public policy, prohibit such gaming activity."

Congress stated that it passed the IGRA in order to provide a statutory basis for Indian gaming; to establish regulations that would be strong enough to exclude organized crime, ensuring that the tribes would be the primary beneficiaries of the gaming operations; and to keep the games fair and honest. To accomplish those goals, IGRA created the National Indian Gambling Commission (NIGC) and put it in charge of tribal gaming.

The IGRA recognizes three classes of gaming: Class I gaming includes social games played for prizes of minimal value, and traditional forms of Native American gaming connected with tribal ceremonies or celebrations. The tribes have exclusive authority to regulate this class of gaming. Class II gaming includes bingo, poker, and lottery-like games such as pull tabs. Class III gaming includes casino games such as blackjack and slot machines, and pari-mutuel wagering.

Before it may offer Class II or Class III gaming, a tribe must meet two basic requirements: First, the state where the tribal land is located must allow such gaming "for any purpose by any person, organization, or entity." Second, the tribal government must pass an ordinance authorizing the gaming.

In order to offer Class II gaming, a tribe also must obtain the NIGC's approval. Before approving a tribal gaming operation, the NIGC must find that the tribe will actually own the gaming operation, that the proposed facility will not harm the public health or safety, that there are adequate safeguards against infiltration by undesirables, and that gaming revenue will go back to tribe members. Once approval is granted, the gaming operation operates under the NIGC's supervision. The NIGC can reject tribal agreements with outside businesses, bar undesirables from the gaming operation, and fine or even shut down a gaming operation that violates the IGRA.

In order to offer Class III gaming, a tribe must enter into a treaty with the state where the tribal land is located. The state must negotiate with the tribe in good faith. Tribal-state compacts address such issues as what games will be offered at the casino, what rules will govern those games (for example, minimum age and maximum bet limits), and who will be in charge of regulating them. Even though tribes are not required to pay state taxes, many compacts provide that the tribe will pay a portion of its gaming revenue to cover the costs of gaming enforcement or to help surrounding communities cope with the added costs of having a casino in the area. A tribe also might turn over part of its revenue for the *exclusive* right to offer a form of gambling. In Connecticut, for example, tribes negotiated for the right to offer slot machines, which are not permitted elsewhere in the state.

The IGRA resulted in a significant unintended consequence: the proliferation of casino-type gaming in states where lawmakers would not have approved it on their own. This happened after the courts ruled that if a state allowed low-stakes casino-type gambling, such as "Las Vegas nights" to benefit charities, it had to allow tribes to build full-fledged casinos. Critics of the IGRA also point out that the act's primary focus was bingo, and that the regulations governing Class III gambling are less stringent than those governing Class II gambling. They add that the law in effect makes the tribes themselves the primary regulators of casino-type gambling.

In hearings held by the National Gambling Impact Study Commission, state officials raised several complaints about the IGRA. They argued that the federal government did too little to enforce the law; that the law required states to negotiate in good faith with tribes, but allowed tribes to start gaming operations without state permission if negotiations went nowhere; and that the definitions of permissible gaming were unclear. The commission agreed with state officials that technological advances had blurred the line between Class II and Class III gambling, and called on Congress to define those classes more precisely.

Jones, the mayor of Las Vegas, complained to the NGISC about convenience gambling in her city. "Children see gambling as part of the same environment as candy and soda," she said.[52] In a 1989 survey of business leaders, only 3 percent considered Las Vegas an attractive place to locate a business.

By contrast, Utah—which has no legalized gambling—advertises itself as a wholesome place to live and work. That state's governor once said during a television interview, "We're the number one job creation state in the country. We're number two in personal income growth. . . . And there are a lot of people, frankly, that would like to move to a state where there is no gaming, where in fact you have a safe place, a clean place to live."[53] Professor Kindt adds, "In the long-term, gambling-free states should experience proportionately fewer personal and business bankruptcies, stronger financial institutions, more vibrant business economies, and better tourist, business, and community environments."[54]

Legalization triggers a "race to the bottom."

A state's decision to legalize gambling sets off a domino effect by putting pressure on other states to follow suit. The NGISC described how lotteries spread from state to state:

> The modern history of lotteries demonstrates that when a state authorizes a lottery, inevitably citizens from neighboring states without lotteries will cross the border to purchase tickets. The apparent loss of potential tax revenues by these latter states often gives rise to demands that they institute lotteries of their own, in order to keep this money in-state, for use at home. Once any of these states installs a lottery, however, the same dynamic will assert itself in still other states further afield.[55]

Competition among states for revenue creates added pressure to expand existing forms of gambling and legalize new ones.

Robert Goodman explains how state lawmakers, like compulsive gamblers, "chase" their losses:

> Politicians begin by legalizing some restricted forms of gambling—pari-mutuel horseracing, or a lottery, or perhaps limited-stake betting in casinos—and then, after watching their initial successes decline, or as they become worried about another state siphoning their gambling dollars, they frenetically start upping the ante. They legalize new games or they get rid of restrictions and betting limits on their old ones. As the chasing process progresses, more hard-core forms of gambling are rapidly legalized in a copycat race by state after state. As each state's gambling menu expands, its gambling policy begins to spin out of control, and governments and state residents soon find themselves with gambling enterprises they never imagined when their process of legalization first began.[56]

Iowa's experience with riverboat gambling is a good example. When it first legalized riverboats, the maximum bet was $5, and a player could not lose more than $200 a day. Soon afterward, other states—most notably, Mississippi—legalized riverboat gambling but placed no limits on bets. The competition forced Iowa lawmakers to choose between repealing the limits or losing business, and possibly even the boats themselves, to other states. They voted to drop the limits.

Gambling interests thwart public opinion.

Gambling interests use their wealth and political influence to get favorable legislation passed. In 1974, New Jersey voters rejected a proposal that would have allowed casinos in the state. Two years later, the casino industry returned with a new proposal. Supporters told the public that casino revenue would be earmarked for the benefit of older residents and promised that gambling regulators would take a hard line against organized crime. More importantly, pro-casino forces outspent their opponents in their campaigning by 60 to 1.

New Jersey was unusual in that voters were given the final say on casinos. In other states, lawmakers approved them even though, as opponents point out, there was no grass-roots movement to legalize and expand gambling, especially casinos. (By contrast, there have been citizen-led movements dedicated, for example, to decriminalizing marijuana and allowing doctor-assisted suicide.) The public has had even less input regarding Indian bingo halls and casinos because the Indian Gaming Regulatory Act (IGRA) leaves states with little alternative but to allow tribes to offer gambling.

A decision to legalize gambling is all but final. Once legalized, gambling creates political constituencies that not only favor keeping it legal but also want to expand it. For example, restaurant owners support slot machines in their establishments in order to recapture the business they lost to casinos, and teachers support expansion of the lottery because lottery revenue is earmarked for education. Gambling interests also reinvest gambling revenue into lobbying. That is true of Indian tribes as well as casino companies. Author Richard Hoffer commented, "One watchdog has said tribes spent $130 million on political contributions in the last six years, influencing legislation in their favor. . . . The tribes, who are becoming the go-to guys with their gambling strike, will be crucial to state politics for years to come."[57]

In fact, the government itself has an interest in keeping gambling legal. Not only is it dependent on gambling for tax dollars; in some cases it has gone into debt to build infrastructure, such as freeway exits and riverboat docks, to bring people to gambling venues. Jeffrey Bloomberg described how Deadwood found itself dependent on casinos: "The city council decided to sell revenue bonds pledging revenues from predicted gaming and sales taxes to finance the improvement. If the citizens of Deadwood wanted to get rid of gambling today they could not do so without total bankruptcy."[58]

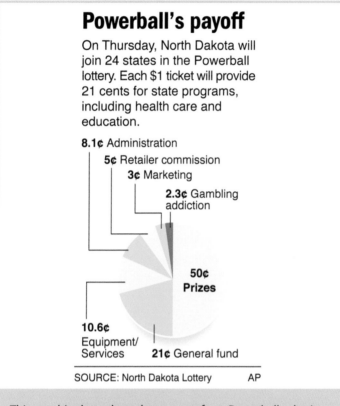

Powerball's payoff

On Thursday, North Dakota will join 24 states in the Powerball lottery. Each $1 ticket will provide 21 cents for state programs, including health care and education.

8.1¢ Administration

5¢ Retailer commission

3¢ Marketing

2.3¢ Gambling addiction

50¢ Prizes

10.6¢ Equipment/ Services

21¢ General fund

SOURCE: North Dakota Lottery   AP

This graphic shows how the revenue from Powerball sales is distributed. Opponents of legalized gambling contend that allowing gambling activities has adverse effects on local economies.

The gambling industry is keenly aware that legalized gambling takes on a life of its own. The industry therefore tries to get "a foot in the door" by persuading lawmakers to approve gambling on a limited basis, and once it succeeds, lobbies to expand gambling. Robert Goodman quotes a lobbyist for the gambling industry as saying, "A good rule of thumb is to look at it as a ladder. Areas that have no gambling at all warm up to the 'cruises to nowhere' [excursions into international waters, where state gambling laws do not apply] as the first rung on the ladder. The next step would be dockside. At the top would be land-based casinos."[59]

The gambling industry acts irresponsibly.

The gambling industry uses sophisticated tactics, including heavy advertising, to attract players. Recently, activists criticized

FROM THE BENCH

Should Casinos Be Liable for Allowing Compulsive Gamblers to Play? *Merrill v. Trump Indiana, Inc.*

Some pathological gamblers, either because they refuse treatment or because they relapse after treatment, end up losing large amounts of money in casinos. Some believe that a pathological gambler should be able to sue a casino that knows of a person's gambling problem but allows that person to gamble anyway.

That argument was the basis of a lawsuit filed by Mark Merrill against Trump Indiana, Inc., the operator of a riverboat casino. Merrill had gone into treatment for compulsive gambling. During his stay in the clinic, his rehabilitation counselor spoke to a representative of Trump Indiana and asked the casino to exclude Merrill. The representative obliged, and Merrill was placed on the casino's "eviction list." Two years later, Merrill relapsed and went back to Trump Indiana, where he lost heavily. In an effort to get money to pay his gambling debts, Merrill robbed two banks. He was caught, found guilty, and sent to prison.

Merrill blamed Trump Indiana for his troubles because it had allowed him to continue gambling. He argued that the casino had entered into a contract to exclude him or, alternatively, that it had a legal duty to keep him out. The District Court rejected all of Merrill's claims. He appealed to the U.S. Court of Appeals for the Seventh Circuit, which, in *Merrill v. Trump Indiana, Inc.*, affirmed the decision. Judge Sarah Barker Evans wrote the court's opinion.

Judge Evans concluded that Trump Indiana was not liable to Merrill for having let him gamble after his counselor asked that he be excluded. She pointed out that at the time Merrill resumed gambling, the Indiana Gaming Commission did not require casinos to maintain a list of excluded players. She added that even if such a requirement had been in effect at the time, a casino that violated it would have had to answer to the gaming commission, not to the compulsive gambler efforts to target Asians and Asian Americans, whose culture has embraced gambling for thousands of years. Timothy Fong, the codirector of the Gambling Studies Program at the University of California, Los Angeles, has noticed an increase in problem gambling among Asians, and he blames aggressive marketing campaigns. "If the casinos singled out African Americans and

who should have been excluded. Given the extent of gambling regulation in Indiana, she concluded that the legislature had not intended to give patrons the right to sue over a violation of state gaming rules.

Judge Evans also concluded that the common law of Indiana imposed no legal duty on Trump Indiana to exclude Merrill. She observed:

The closest analogy to Merrill's situation is that of a tavern's liability to exercise reasonable care to protect its patrons. In Indiana, a tavern proprietor serving alcohol can be held liable, under certain conditions, if an intoxicated patron injures another patron or a third party....But a patron who drives while intoxicated, causing his own injuries, cannot recover from the tavern that served him alcohol.

Some argue that it would be unfair to hold casinos liable for allowing players like Merrill to gamble. They point out that it is more difficult for a casino employee to recognize a compulsive gambler than it is for a bartender to recognize a customer who has had too much to drink. They also contend that gamblers are adults and therefore have a responsibility to avoid putting themselves in a situation where they can lose control.

In Nevada, which has more casinos than any other state, gamblers such as Merrill may not use compulsive gambling as a defense against having to pay gambling debts. Section 463.368(6) of the Nevada Revised Statutes provides:

"A patron's claim of having a mental or behavioral disorder involving gambling:

(a) Is not a defense in any action by a [casino] licensee or a person acting on behalf of a licensee to enforce a credit instrument or the debt that the credit instrument represents.
(b) Is not a valid counterclaim to such an action."

marketed to them as heavily as they do Asians, I'd imagine there'd be this huge political outcry," he said.[60]

Once players enter a casino, they find themselves in an environment where they can easily lose their inhibitions. Carl Bechtold, an opponent of legalized gambling, explains:

> Gambling environments, specifically within casinos, are scientifically and socially designed to transport players beyond the realm of rational decisions. Presentations by one prominent international researcher concluded ... [that having] strong emotional/physiological responses during a session of play is a natural human experience. The expectation that the player will be able to continue to make controlled, informed, rational decisions during such a session of continuous gambling is ill-founded."[61]

The gambling industry has also been criticized for making it too easy to bet with borrowed money. To begin with, casinos themselves offer short-term loans called "casino markers." In 1997, Atlantic City's casinos alone issued some $2.13 billion in markers. Other players gamble with cash advances on their credit cards. The NGISC found that "the easy availability of automated teller machines (ATMs) and credit machines encourages some gamblers to wager more than they intended," and recommended that "states, tribal governments, and pari-mutuel facilities ban credit card cash advance machines and other devices activated by debit or credit cards from the immediate area where gambling takes place."[62]

Furthermore, casinos have been accused of doing too little to curb problem gambling. The courts have generally held that casinos have no legal duty to stop compulsive gamblers from playing. (By contrast, a bar owner can be found liable for continuing to serve an intoxicated customer.) Nevada went one step further and passed a law[63] that bars a losing gambler from raising his or her gambling-related disorder as a defense against paying a gambling debt.

Summary

The gambling industry is highly profitable, but it has profited at the expense of the rest of society. Contrary to the industry's claims, legalized gambling does little to stimulate the local economy in many communities, and in some communities it has hurt local businesses and residents. The gambling industry has used its wealth and influence to overcome public resistance. The initial decision to legalize gambling leads to the eventual legalization of new forms of gambling. In an effort to attract business and maximize profits, casino companies encourage problem gambling and at the same time shift gambling-related costs to the rest of society.

Legalized Gaming Benefits States and Communities

L egalized gaming proponent Richard Hoffer commented on the pastime's popularity in the United States: "You think this is Fast Food Nation? We Americans bet each other about $80 billion last year, more than we spent on movie tickets, CDs, theme parks, spectator sports, and video games—combined!"[64] Once described as a "pariah industry" because of its association with organized crime and prostitution, legalized gaming is now an accepted form of recreation. Many Americans recognize that gaming also has a positive economic impact on communities, and that it can enhance the quality of life for gamers and non-gamers alike.

Gaming is mainstream entertainment.
One reason why laws against gaming remained on the books for so long is that gaming was perceived as deviant behavior and associated with drifters and underworld figures. Vicki Abt and

her coauthors observe, however, that "if gambling were truly deviant, if racetracks and lotteries and casinos did not satisfy a widely and deeply rooted demand, the problems created by gambling would be trivial, and confined to the small segment of the population liable to become compulsive gamblers."[65]

Gaming began to lose its stigma after World War II, when racetracks offered middle-class Americans a day of entertainment that included pari-mutuel betting. That trend accelerated during the 1950s, when Las Vegas reinvented itself as a destination for middle-class vacationers and business travelers. Today, "as the city's annual visitation climbed toward 40 million, Las Vegas casino operators relished their success in transcending the stigma formerly attached to gambling, and had successfully established Las Vegas as a destination for all seasons and temperaments."[66] Las Vegas calls itself the "entertainment capital of the world," and its casino hotels earn more revenue from non-gaming activities such as dining, shopping, and shows than they do from gaming itself.

Gaming is now firmly established as mainstream entertainment. It is primarily social in nature: Researchers have found that the majority of casino patrons go as part of a group, and it is popular with middle-aged, middle-class Americans. According to a recent survey commissioned by Harrah's Entertainment, the average casino guest is a 46-year-old woman from a household with an above-average income. In 1975, researchers at the University of Michigan asked bettors why they gambled. Their answers: 86 percent of racetrack bettors and 78 percent of casino bettors said that they gambled "to have a good time." Bettors told the Michigan researchers that "excitement" and "challenge" were more common motivations than "to make money," which was mentioned by 33 percent of racetrack and 36 percent of casino patrons.

Gaming brings pleasure to millions of Americans and enhances the quality of their lives. "Losses incurred as a result of conventional gambling are voluntary expenditures for a particular leisure activity," explain Vicki Abt and colleagues. "They do not differ in sociological meaning from expenditures for movie or theater tickets, pleasure travel, an evening at Carnegie Hall, a night's dancing at a discotheque, or a day's amusement at Disneyland."[67]

It has been argued that in spite of the odds against winning, gamers behave rationally. That is so because the entertainment associated with gaming is worth the money lost. Abt and her coauthors observe: "Money heightens player involvement and provides an easy measure of outcomes, but gain or loss is not always or even usually the primary motivation. Players gamble *with* but not always *for* money."[68] It has been argued that even lottery players, who face the worst odds in legalized gaming, act rationally. Benedict Carey, a science reporter at the *New York Times*, explains:

> Like a throwaway lifestyle magazine, lottery tickets engage transforming fantasies: a wine cellar, a pool, a vision of tropical blues and white sand. The difference is that the ticket can deliver.
>
> And as long as the fantasy is possible, even a negligible probability of winning becomes paradoxically reinforcing.[69]

Carey also reported that the mere possibility of winning the lottery brings pleasure: "In brain-imaging studies of . . . healthy adults placing bets, neuroscientists have found that the prospect of a reward activates the same circuits in the brain that the payoffs themselves do.[70]

Gaming helps the poorest Americans.

Before they offered gaming, Indian tribes had few economic options and many Native Americans lived in extreme poverty. As Justice Byron White said in the decision for the 1987 case *California v. Cabazon Band of Mission Indians*:

> The Cabazon and Morongo Reservations contain no natural resources which can be exploited. The tribal games at present provide the sole source of revenues for the operation of the tribal governments and the provision of tribal services. They are also the major sources of employment on the reservations. Self-determination and economic development are not within reach if the Tribes cannot raise revenues and provide employment for their members. The Tribes' interests obviously parallel the federal interests.[71]

Since the Indian Gaming Regulation Act (IGRA) became law, many tribes have become prosperous. The best-known example is the Pequot, a tribal nation that was almost exterminated by colonial settlers in the seventeenth century. Its survivors were relegated to land in eastern Connecticut that no one else wanted. After IGRA took effect, the Pequot negotiated a compact with the state of Connecticut to build Foxwoods Resort Casino, the second largest property in the world. Foxwoods "now has 6,300 slot machines on nearly 7 acres of floor space, a Michael Jordan Steakhouse, a WNBA team (the Connecticut Sun plays in its 10,000-seat arena), its own planetarium, and a 34-story hotel with 1,200 rooms."[72] Revenue from the casino, about $1 billion per year, is distributed to members of the tribal nation under a profit-sharing system. Every Pequot who is at least 18 years old receives a monthly payment that averages out to about $100,000 per year. He or she is also guaranteed a job, free medical care, day care, and tuition at any private school or college.

Even though the National Gambling Impact Study Commission (NGISC) opposes the expansion of legalized gaming, it conceded that the industry has helped Native Americans:

> Through gambling, tribes have been able to provide employment to their members and other residents where the federal policies failed to create work. This has resulted in dramatic

drops in the extraordinarily high unemployment rates in many, though not all, communities in Indian country and a reduction in welfare rolls and other governmental services for the unemployed.[73]

Gaming revenue has funded tribal courts, police and fire departments, roads, land-use planning, education, housing, public health programs, and the preservation of languages and cultures.

Are Gambling Debts Collectable?

Until recently, the law clearly stated that gambling debts were not collectible. This legal rule dates back to 1710, when England adopted the Statute of Anne. It provided:

> All notes, bills, bonds, judgments, mortgages, or other securities or conveyances whatsoever given, granted, drawn or entered into, or executed by any person or persons whatsoever, where the whole, or any part of the consideration of such conveyances or securities shall be for any money, or other valuable thing whatsoever, won by gaming, or playing at cards, dice, tables, tennis, bowls, or other game or games whatsoever, or by betting on the sides or hands of such as do game at any of the games aforesaid, or for the reimbursing or repaying any money knowingly lent or advanced at the time and place of such play, to any person or persons so gaming or betting as aforesaid, or that shall, during such play, so play or bet, shall be utterly void, frustrate, and of none effect, to all intents and purposes whatsoever.

Parliament passed the law because many of England's aristocrats were gambling and losing heavily, and their losses were disrupting the country's land-based society. In essence, the Statute of Anne was intended to protect wealthy landowners from their own foolishness by barring winners from going to court to collect gambling debts.

After the statute was passed, courts treated gambling debts in the same manner as it treated contracts involving illegal drugs or prostitution: It "left the parties where it found them" and refused to hear the case. That approach appealed to

It has also funded nongaming business ventures that will diversify and strengthen tribal economies in the future. This might not have been possible without gaming because the federal government has a history of underfunding tribes. Robert Loescher, a Native American who served in the NGISC, summed up the impact of tribal gaming: "Indian gaming furthers Indian Self Determination through tribal ownership and control of its gaming operations. It furthers economic benefit to the surrounding

---

many people's moral sensibilities—believing that the law should not lend a hand to illegal behavior—but it also opened the door to the use of violence to collect debts and settle other disputes.

The Statute of Anne became part of the common law of every state, in part because of colonial and state lawmakers' hostility toward gambling. Even though legislation can alter or even abolish common-law rules, antigambling forces prevailed upon state lawmakers to leave the rule in force.

When Nevada legalized gambling in 1931, it did not repeal the Statute of Anne. At first, the state's gaming industry learned to live with the statute. In the early days of legal gaming, casinos used strong-arm tactics to collect debts—a practice that was apparently tolerated by local authorities. Later, after corporations entered the gaming business, casino companies collected debts either by obtaining payment from the player's bank or by barring the player from gambling until he or she paid up.

Competition from Atlantic City, along with a Nevada court decision that required casinos to treat outstanding loans to players as income, led the gaming industry to ask lawmakers to create a mechanism for collecting debts. The result was a piece of legislation passed in 1983 that established a procedure for collecting from bettors who refuse to pay. An important requirement of the law is that the debt be put down in writing—for example, as a "casino marker," a document that looks like a check and is signed by the bettor. The law does not allow a bettor to take a disputed debt to court. However, a bettor can complain to the Nevada Gaming Control Board if he or she believes that a casino did not play by the rules. Presumably, a casino would not want to risk the bad publicity—let alone the possibility of losing its gaming license—on account of having cheated a player.

Gaming money sees dramatic rise

Revenue from Indian gambling locations has more than tripled since 1995. Currently 28 states have tribes with gambling operations, according to National Indian Gaming Commission.

Indian gaming revenue

$20 billion
16
12
8
4
0

$18.5
$5.5

'95   '00   '04*

Number of gaming tribes by state

| 1-5 | 6-10 | 11-19 | More than 20 |

NOTE: States shown in white have no gaming tribes. Number of tribes not exhaustive because gaming facilities open and close over time. *Revenue for 2004 from the National Indian Gaming Association, remaining numbers from NIGC

SOURCES: NIGA, NIGC   AP

The chart above shows how much revenue from Native American gambling has risen in recent years. The map shows the number of gaming tribes per state.

communities by employing at least 100,000 people regardless of race, color, or creed."[74]

Indian gaming helps surrounding communities by generating economic activity and employing local residents. According to the National Indian Gaming Association (NIGA), two-thirds of gaming jobs are held by non–Native Americans.

There are many examples of increased economic activity due to gaming. One of those is Avoyelles Parish in Louisiana. It was one of the state's poorest until the Tunica-Biloxi Tribe built the Paragon Casino and Resort. The parish's unemployment rate fell from 8.4 percent in 1996 to 4.7 percent in 2006. In California's Del Norte County, one of that state's poorest, the Tolowa Tribe opened the Elk Valley Rancheria and Casino, which provided more than 5,000 new jobs. Revenue from the casino helped finance a $35 million wastewater treatment plant in the county.

Gaming produces jobs and generates tax revenue.

The gaming industry contributes to the economy of those states and communities where it is permitted. Because it is labor intensive, the industry generates a substantial number of jobs. The American Gaming Association (AGA) estimates that commercial casinos employ more than 354,000 people nationwide and generate an additional 450,000 jobs in related businesses. The NIGA estimates that tribal gaming has led to the creation of more than a half a million jobs. According to recent estimates by the AGA and NIGA, commercial casinos paid $11 billion in wages and benefits and tribal casinos paid $6 million. That money has enabled employees to buy homes, cars, and large appliances, and pay for other major life expenses. It has also reduced the government's unemployment compensation and public assistance costs. The NGISC recognized the gaming industry's contribution, finding that, "unlike many industries, casino gambling creates full-time, entry-level jobs, which are badly needed in communities suffering from chronic unemployment and underemployment. Dozens of casino workers testified that these economic benefits are felt in the home and not just at city hall."[75]

The NGISC also heard testimony that casinos offered better-quality jobs in terms of higher pay and better health and pension benefits than comparable jobs in the service sector. That testimony was consistent with a 1996 economic impact study by Andersen Consulting, which found that gaming industry employees earned higher average salaries than their counterparts

Credit Cards and Online Gambling

Most Americans who gamble online use credit cards to open an account with gambling sites. Some unlucky players have later tried to avoid paying by arguing that their debts arose out of illegal behavior and therefore their creditors had no right to sue them.

One early case was *Providian National Bank v. Haines*. In 1998, Providian sued Cynthia Haines, who had lost more than $70,000 gambling online with her credit cards. Haines responded to the lawsuit by countersuing the bank. She argued that the bank had engaged in unfair business practices and, in addition, had aided and abetted a crime by doing business with illegal gambling Web sites. (At the time, all casino gambling was illegal in Haines's home state of California.) Haines demanded her money back, as well as a court order barring banks and card issuers from collecting gambling debts from other California residents. The case was settled before it went to trial. Under the settlement, Providian forgave all of Haines's gambling debts and paid nearly $225,000 of her attorney's fees. After Haines's case was settled, many banks stopped doing business with online casinos out of fear that the courts would not allow them to collect gambling debts from cardholders.

Other losing gamblers have taken a different approach. Larry Thompson, a resident of Kansas, and Lawrence Bradley, a resident of New Hampshire, used their credit cards to open accounts at offshore casinos. Ultimately, Thompson lost a total of $1,510, and Bradley lost a total of $7,048. Both men went to court to avoid paying. They argued that the banks had participated in a gambling enterprise by allowing cardholders to use the cards to open accounts and by allowing their corporate logos to appear on casinos' Web sites. The men also argued that the banks had illegally "collected gambling debts" by billing them for what they spent for casino credits.

Thompson's and Bradley's cases were based on the Racketeer Influenced and Corrupt Organizations Act of 1970 (RICO), a complicated federal law that in the motion picture industry, other amusement and recreation sectors, and the hotel industry. Furthermore, many casino employees are labor union members, who tend to earn more money and enjoy greater job security than nonunion employees.

was intended to stop organized crime from infiltrating legitimate businesses. A violation of RICO requires proof of either a "pattern of racketeering activity" or the collection of an unlawful debt. A "pattern of racketeering activity," in turn, requires proof of two "predicate acts"—that is, separate crimes under either federal or state law. Even though RICO is a criminal statute, it also permits victims to sue racketeers and receive three times the damages they had suffered.

These cases, along with those of 21 others who had filed similar claims against their banks, were consolidated in the U.S. District Court for the Eastern District of Louisiana. Thompson's and Bradley's cases were chosen as "test cases" and tried together. The District Court ruled in the banks' favor, and Thompson and Bradley appealed. In *In re Mastercard International, Inc., Internet Gambling Litigation,* the U.S. Court of Appeals for the Fifth Circuit affirmed the lower court's judgment. Judge James Dennis wrote the court's opinion.

Judge Dennis first concluded that the banks had engaged in no predicate acts that would trigger liability under RICO. He found that the banks had not violated the gambling laws of either Kansas or New Hampshire by extending credit to be used for gambling. In addition, he found that the banks had not violated the Wire Act because Thompson and Bradley had played casino games and the Wire Act applied only to sports betting. Because the Wire Act did not apply to online casinos, Judge Dennis also found that the banks had not falsely represented to Thompson and Bradley that what they were doing was legal. Finally, because neither federal law nor the laws of their home states prohibited them from placing bets online, the court found that Thompson's and Bradley's debts were lawful. Judge Dennis also scolded the plaintiffs. He wrote:

Thompson and Bradley simply are not victims under the facts of these cases. Rather, as the district court wrote, "they are independent actors who made a knowing and voluntary choice to engage in a course of conduct." In engaging in this conduct, they got exactly what they bargained for—gambling "chips" with which they could place wagers.

John Wilhelm, the head of one of Nevada's largest labor unions and a member of the NGISC, posed the following question: "Those who oppose legal gambling have a moral obligation to answer: If they would deny a good Union job to a family trapped in poverty because they oppose gambling, what alternative will they offer that family?"[76]

Gaming generates a substantial amount of revenue for states and cities that allow it. According to AGA figures, commercial casinos paid more than $5.2 billion in taxes in 2006. Nevada alone collected $1.013 billion from commercial casinos that year; and in fact gaming revenue accounts for one-third of that state's general fund revenues. Indiana was second, taking in $833.7 million in gaming revenue, followed by Illinois with $830.2 million. Detroit's casinos paid the city more than $171 million in taxes and fees. That same year, Atlantic City's casinos contributed $417 million to a New Jersey state fund for older and disabled residents and paid an additional $65 million into a special fund aimed at combating blight.

The government also benefits from forms of gaming other than that of commercial casinos. During fiscal year 2005, states took in $14.5 billion in lottery revenue, bringing the grand total to more than $200 billion since the first ticket was sold in New Hampshire in 1964. "Racinos" paid a total of $1.44 billion in taxes, including $445.6 million in West Virginia alone. The NIGA estimated that in 2004, casinos and businesses associated with them paid $5.5 billion in Social Security and other federal taxes. Even though Native American tribes do not have to pay state taxes, tribal gaming operations paid $1.8 billion to the states under the terms of tribal-state compacts, as well as $100 million to local governments.

Gaming benefits hard-hit communities.

Officials from a number of struggling communities told the NGISC that the quality of life had improved after casinos arrived. Atlantic City Mayor James Whalen said that his city would have died had it not been for casinos. The commission agreed with those officials. It found: "Indeed, a number of communities plagued by high unemployment have found a form of economic renewal through gambling, particularly through the development of 'destination resorts.'"[77]

Detroit is a notable success story. In spite of warnings that it would bring crime and economic blight, casino gaming has helped the city. In September 2007, the *Detroit Free Press* reported: "Since opening, the Detroit casinos have pumped just over $1 billion into the city coffers and created about 7,000 jobs at a time when many Michigan companies are closing or cutting back."[78] It added, "The downtown crime rate two years ago was 2,559 incidents for every 100,000 people. In 2001, the rate was 4,089 per 100,000 people."[79] In late 2007, Detroit's casinos moved from temporary facilities into luxury casino-hotel complexes that represent a combined investment of $1.5 billion. This new construction will help give Detroit's casinos "destination" status and increase their contribution to the local economy.

French Lick, Indiana, is another example. During the 1920s, it was a resort where people drank bootleg whisky and gambled in back rooms. The Great Depression, followed by a crackdown on gaming in the state, crippled the local economy. A *New York Times* story noted that French Lick had three liquor stores but no grocery store, and most of its downtown shops were vacant. Gaming—this time, legal—was expected to help revive the community:

> Of the 1,013 resort employees who have already been hired, 566 are from Orange County. There are $15 million worth of public works projects in the pipeline, including a $5.5 million downtown revitalization.
>
> Because of its share of casino revenue, French Lick will work with an estimated annual budget of $4 million per year, up from $900,000.[80]

Gaming provides some insurance against economic down-
turns. During recessions, traditional sources of revenue such
as sales and income taxes fall off, forcing governments to look

FROM THE BENCH

High Court Allows Casino Advertising: *Greater New Orleans Broadcasting Association v. United States*

Title 18, §1304 of the U.S. Code, a provision of the Communications Act of 1934, made it illegal to broadcast advertisements for "any lottery, gift enterprise, or similar scheme, offering prizes dependent in whole or in part upon lot or chance." This ban was the result of lingering anti-lottery sentiment in the United States at the time. Later, the courts applied the ban to advertising by casinos.

Beginning in the 1970s, however, the public became more tolerant of gambling. As a result, Congress amended §1304 in 1975 to allow advertising of lotteries in states where they were legal, and amended it again in 1988 to allow advertising of tribal gaming and games operated by charities. Still, §1304 prohibited the advertising of gambling in those states where it was illegal.

A group of broadcasters wished to run advertisements for casinos located in Louisiana and Mississippi, where they were legal. The Federal Communications Commission, which was primarily responsible for enforcing §1304, told the broadcasters that doing so would violate the law because the advertisements would also reach audiences in Arkansas and Texas, where casinos were illegal.

The broadcasters filed suit against the government, arguing that §1304 violated their right to commercial free speech under the First Amendment. The government countered that §1304 was constitutional because it restricted speech in order to achieve two worthwhile purposes: discouraging casinos from enticing problem gamblers into their establishments, and helping states without casinos to restrict gaming within their own borders.

The district court ruled that §1304 was constitutional, and a federal appeals court affirmed that ruling. However, in two other challenges to §1304, courts elsewhere in the country came to the opposite conclusion. In order to resolve the conflict, the U.S. Supreme Court took up the broadcasters' appeal. In 1999 in *Greater New Orleans Broadcasting Association v. United States*, the justices unanimously concluded that §1304's casino advertising ban was unconstitutional.

Justice John Paul Stevens wrote the court's opinion. He first found that the advertisements concerned lawful activities and were not misleading. He also found that even though casinos generated social costs, those costs were offset—and elsewhere for revenues. Gaming is one such source because it is "counter-cyclical." In other words, people are at least as likely, if not more so, to take part in gaming during hard times. Thanks

---

sometimes outweighed—by the benefits of gaming. Noting that the federal government had encouraged Native American tribes to go into the gaming business, he observed that "the federal policy of discouraging gambling in general, and casino gambling in particular, is now decidedly equivocal."

Justice Stevens next concluded that the government had failed to prove that banning casino advertising was the least-restrictive means of limiting the social costs of casino gaming. He wrote:

While it is no doubt fair to assume that more advertising would have some impact on overall demand for gambling, it is also reasonable to assume that much of that advertising would merely channel gamblers to one casino rather than another. More important, any measure of the effectiveness of the Government's attempt to minimize the social costs of gambling cannot ignore Congress's simultaneous encouragement of tribal casino gambling, which may well be growing at a rate exceeding any increase in gambling or compulsive gambling that private casino advertising could produce.

Justice Stevens added that the enforcement of §1304 had become so inconsistent that the law could no longer stand up to a First Amendment challenge. The law's principal inconsistency was that it imposed different restrictions on tribal casinos than it did on commercial casinos, even though both offered similar games and generated similar social costs.

Finally, Justice Stevens observed that forms of regulation unrelated to speech would more effectively reduce the social costs of gambling than would a ban of advertising. He suggested "a prohibition or supervision of gambling on credit; limitations on the use of cash machines on casino premises; controls on admissions; pot or betting limits; location restrictions; and licensing requirements."

There were two concurring opinions. Chief Justice William Rehnquist agreed that §1304 imposed inconsistent restrictions, but argued that Congress still could have saved it from a First Amendment challenge had it attempted to regulate the gaming industry itself rather than the manner in which the industry advertised. Justice Clarence Thomas agreed that §1304 was unconstitutional, but on broader grounds—namely, that laws intended "to keep legal users of a product or service ignorant in order to manipulate their choices in the marketplace" were per se unconstitutional.

to the gaming industry, Las Vegas weathered the recession of the early 1990s better than most cities. Gaming can also lessen the impact of business closures elsewhere in the area. The Fox-woods Casino, which employs 10,000 people, cushioned eastern Connecticut's economy when help was most needed: The open-ing of Foxwoods coincided with the end of the Cold War, which meant less work for Electric Boat and other local defense indus-try contractors.

The gaming industry also played a role in the Gulf Coast's recovery after Hurricane Katrina devastated the area. Two years after the storm hit, Leonard Blackwell, the former chairman of the Mississippi Gaming Commission, wrote:

During the past 24 months the industry has:

- Reopened 10 properties along the Mississippi Gulf Coast, and the Hard Rock Hotel and Casino;

- Invested nearly $1.4 billion for reconstruction on the Mississippi Coast; [and]

- Brought nearly 20,000 gaming industry employees back to work.[81]

Blackwell also cited an AGA-commissioned survey of com-munity leaders in the Gulf Coast. Of those surveyed, 65 percent said that casino companies in their area "very much helped" in aiding the local recovery.

Summary

Gaming, once branded as a vice, is now considered a mainstream form of recreation. A majority of American adults take part in it, and most do so for entertainment and social interaction, not to make money. Tribal gaming has helped Native Americans escape poverty and become self-sufficient, and has benefited non-tribe members as well. Casinos have created hundreds of thousands of jobs, many of them well paying. Casinos have helped revive communities that had fallen on hard times or suffered from natural disasters, and they have lessened the impact of recessions. Gaming also makes a substantial contribution to government programs. Every year, states take in billions of dollars in lottery revenue as well as billions more in taxes paid by gaming companies and their employees.

Government Promotion of Gambling Is Bad Policy

A new era in legalized gambling began on March 12, 1964, when New Hampshire Governor John King bought the state's first sweepstakes ticket. Modest as it was, the New Hampshire Lottery transformed the government from a licensing middleman into an active participant in the gambling industry.

In recent years, states have become more deeply involved in gambling. The Indian Gaming Regulatory Act (IGRA), which gave tribes the legal right to open casinos, left states with little choice but to enter into compacts allowing them. Some states capitalized on the IGRA and allowed tribes to offer additional forms of gambling in exchange for a portion of the proceeds.

The states' involvement in gambling raises serious ethical questions. As the National Gambling Impact Study Commission (NGISC) noted, "Some observers have alleged that, as a result, considerations of public welfare at best take second place. This has often been cast as an inherent conflict of interest: How can a state government ensure that its pursuit of revenues does not conflict with its responsibility to protect the public?"[82] Even among supporters of legalized gambling, there is unease over the government's involvement in a business that for much of the nation's history was considered harmful.

Promoting gambling is different than merely permitting it.

A combination of antigambling sentiment and widespread corruption by private operators led to a nationwide ban on lotteries by the end of the nineteenth century. When the question of relegalization arose, state lawmakers concluded that the public would be more likely to accept the lottery if the government ran the game and the revenue went into the state treasury. The idea was well intentioned but, as David Schwartz observed, "at first looking merely to replace existing illegal gambling, states soon moved into the business of promoting betting and wagering."[83]

Critics point out that the states have shifted from merely offering a lottery to actually encouraging the public to buy tickets. For example, Rebecca Paul Hargrove, the head of Tennessee's lottery, recently said, "Anytime you buy gas, I want you to spend the change on a lottery ticket . . . That's what I do. I raise the money, and the state spends it."[84] Tennessee is not alone in promoting its lottery. According to the North American Association of State and Provincial Lotteries (NASPL), states spent $400 million in 1997 on lottery advertising. That figure is likely higher today because more states have lotteries and states that have long held lotteries have introduced new games. Some believe that at a time when states are struggling to fund programs such as health care and education, advertising the lottery is a misuse of taxpayers' money.

In an effort to maximize revenue, states have made lottery tickets widely available. The NASPL estimates that there are 240,000 retailers selling lottery tickets in the United States. Many of them are located in poor urban neighborhoods. In some states, vending machines in family-oriented businesses such as supermarkets sell tickets costing as much as $20. The easy availability of tickets appears to encourage underage bettors to buy them.

Casino "Self-Exclusion" Laws

Some casino states have passed laws that allow compulsive gamblers to put their names on a "self-exclusion" list that bars them from casinos. Michigan is one such state. A provision of that state's gaming laws, Section 432.225 of the Michigan Compiled Laws, allows gamblers to voluntarily exclude themselves from casinos.

The law directs the Michigan Gaming Control Board to create a list of "disassociated persons." An individual who goes on the list remains there for life because the psychiatric community believes that pathological gambling is a disorder that requires lifelong treatment. To go on the list, a person must complete an application that contains personal information (such as a photograph and physical description) that would allow casino personnel to identify the person, as well as a statement that the person believes that he or she is a problem gambler and is seeking treatment.

The law directs the gaming control board to distribute the disassociated persons list to casinos, the attorney general, and the state police. Casinos must keep a computerized record of those persons who are on the list. A casino may not extend credit, offer check-cashing privileges, or in any way advertise to people on the list.

If a person on the list is found inside a casino, the casino must immediately eject that person and report the incident to the county prosecutor. The person is guilty of criminal trespassing, which is punishable by up to one year in jail and a fine of up to $1,000. In addition, the person's winnings will be confiscated and paid into the state's Compulsive Gaming Prevention Fund. The person cannot sue the state or a casino for its actions in enforcing the law.

Supporters argue that self-exclusion laws provide problem gamblers with an extra incentive to avoid dangerous situations, and also discourage casinos from taking advantage of vulnerable players. Opponents argue that these laws open the door to prohibition, and point out that the gaming industry already encourages casinos to offer voluntary self-exclusion programs. Some also question whether it is good policy to allow citizens to "outsource" self-discipline to the state.

According to the NGISC, "one survey in Minnesota of 15- to 18-year-olds found that 27 percent had purchased lottery tickets. Even higher levels of 32 percent, 34 percent, and 35 percent were recorded in Louisiana, Texas, and Connecticut, respectively."[85]

States deceive the public about lotteries.

An important function of government is to protect citizens from deception and exploitation, but critics contend that state lotteries take advantage of their citizens. To begin with, lotteries offer much worse odds than other forms of legalized gambling. The typical lottery pays out 50 cents in prize money for every dollar wagered. By contrast, racetracks pay out slightly more than 80 cents; slot machines pay out in the 90-cent range; and depending on the bet, craps and blackjack pay out more than 95 cents. Author Richard Hoffer favors legalized gambling, but nevertheless conceded that "a lottery is gambling at its worst, in other words, a system of public taxation gussied up in marketing campaigns and ridiculous catchphrases."[86]

Some lottery advertisements contain statements that, if made by a private business, could violate laws regarding truth in advertising. New York State promoted its lottery with the phrase "All You Need Is a Dollar and a Dream." A much-criticized advertisement for the Illinois Lottery suggested to residents of a low-income Chicago neighborhood that playing the lottery might be "your ticket out of here." The NGISC said, "While the Federal Trade Commission requires statements about probability of winning in commercial sweepstakes games, there is no such federal requirement for lotteries. Lottery advertising rarely explains the poor odds of winning. Many advertisements imply that the odds of winning are even 'better than you might think.'"[87]

Advertising also overstates the lottery's contribution to state programs. Many states tell their citizens that lottery revenue supports the schools. For example, the Michigan State Lottery uses the slogan "You Play, Schools Win," and boasts that it has raised more than $12 billion for schools. That claim is literally true, but it counts revenue dating back to 1972, when the lottery began. In fiscal year 2005, the lottery's contribution to the state's School Aid Fund amounted to only 5 percent of Michigan's spending on public education. In New York, a 1998 report from the state comptroller put it about as bluntly as possible, without actually calling for a refund: "By dedicating it to education, there is an implied promise that the lottery will increase school aid . . . This has never happened in New York . . . Lottery money has never supplemented state aid; it doesn't today and it likely never will . . . In New York, as in many other states, lottery earnings have been earmarked for education primarily as a public relations device."[88]

State-sponsored gambling exploits citizens.

Today's state-sponsored gambling bears little resemblance to the original New Hampshire sweepstakes. Robert Goodman explains why: "After the initial enthusiasm, player interest will wane and government revenues will flatten. But as the states become more dependent on these gambling revenues, they will continue looking for new forms of betting to revive player interest."[89] State lotteries have expanded their operations to include instant games, which some describe as "paper slot machines." There are also new electronic games that have more in common with slot machines than drawings for prizes. When the New York Lottery introduced the new "Quick Draw" game, players considered it so addictive that they began calling it "Lotto Crack." Electronic games are largely confined to adults-only locations such as bars, but those locations might make the problem worse. "In many cases, the element of alcohol is added to the equation, as people sit in bars, nursing their drinks and playing for hours at a time," Goodman notes.[90]

According to the NGISC, convenience gambling is the most detrimental form of legalized gambling. Goodman argues that it exploits not only individuals but the business community as well:

By relying on convenience gambling for economic development, government is staking a claim to compete head to head with other local businesses for the available consumer dollars. But since these other businesses don't have the same advantages and coercive powers that governments have, they are now competing at a clear disadvantage. And since governments have created monopoly-like enterprises out of once formerly criminalized activities, they can make themselves, or their licensees, the sole suppliers of a product.[91]

Convenience gambling might bring short-term economic benefits to the state but may in the long run cause the tax base to shrink.

Finally, once a state creates a lottery, it faces irresistible pressure to legalize other, more aggressive forms of gambling, argue critics such as John Warren Kindt. Connecticut is one example. In the early 1970s, Connecticut instituted a lottery as an alternative to a state income tax. In the years that followed, it legalized pari-mutuel betting and "simulcasts" (betting on races in other locales), and entered into compacts with Native American tribes that opened huge casinos. By 1993, gambling could no longer raise the money needed to fund the state's programs, and lawmakers passed a state income tax.

The lottery is a tax on the poor.

During the eighteenth century, the British government tried to limit participation in the lottery to people who could afford to lose. Tickets were priced at £10, which translates into more than $2,500 in today's money. Nowadays the opposite is true. Tickets are cheap and widely available, especially in low-income urban neighborhoods. Data compiled by state lotteries suggest that a small part of the population, as little as 20 percent, buys a large majority of tickets. Even though the NGISC stopped short of accusing lottery officials of targeting the poor and members of minority groups, it expressed concern about how the game was marketed. It recommended that states with lotteries "reduce their sales dependence on low-income neighborhoods and heavy players in a variety of ways, including limiting advertising and number of sales outlets in low-income areas."[92]

Over the years, supporters of lotteries have defended them as a "voluntary tax," imposed only on those who choose to buy a ticket. Critics reject that notion. "There is hardly much free choice when jobs are scarce or don't pay well, and when government

FROM THE BENCH

What Should the Legal Gambling Age Be?
Latour v. State of Louisiana

In 1998, the Louisiana legislature raised the legal age for buying lottery tickets and playing video poker from 18 to 21. Eugene Latour, a 20-year-old, attempted to buy a lottery ticket at one establishment and play video poker at another, but was turned down both times because he was underage. Latour, along with the owners of the establishments that had refused him, challenged the age limit in court. They argued that by singling out people 18, 19, and 20 years old, the new law violated Article I, §3 of the state's constitution, which outlawed arbitrary discrimination on the basis of age.

This lawsuit was not the first challenge to a 21-year-old age limit in Louisiana. In 1995, that state's highest court held that raising the legal drinking age from 18 to 21 did not violate Article I, §3, because reducing the number of alcohol-related traffic crashes involving young adults was an important enough objective to justify treating them differently.

Latour's challenge went up to the Supreme Court of Louisiana, which in *Latour v. State of Louisiana* unanimously ruled in the state's favor. Justice Bernette Johnson wrote the court's opinion. She observed that as far back as 1879, the state constitution defined gambling as a "vice." The state supreme court interpreted that provision as less than a complete ban, and ruled that the legislature could legalize and regulate certain forms of gambling. In the early 1990s, after energy prices collapsed and the state's economy went into a recession, lawmakers legalized cruise ship and riverboat gambling, a land-based casino in New Orleans, and video poker statewide.

and private casino companies spend hundreds of millions of dollars on behavior modification studies and advertising to tell people they can change their lives through gambling," Goodman argues.[93]

Some opponents also call the lottery an unfair "regressive" tax—that is, one that takes a larger percentage of the income of poor citizens than from wealthier citizens. Critics point out that the poorest members of society spend the highest percentage of

Turning to the age limit, Justice Johnson agreed with the state that preventing young adults from becoming pathological gamblers, protecting the public welfare in general, and ensuring the integrity of legalized gaming were "appropriate governmental purposes." She next concluded that a higher age limit substantially furthered the government's objectives.

Justice Johnson cited the testimony of Dr. James Westphal, a psychiatrist. Westphal stated that 18- to 20-year-olds accounted for 8.2 percent of the total adult population but 22.5 percent of adults who had gambling disorders. In 1998, problem gamblers cost the state of Louisiana $480 million; young adults accounted for $100 million of that sum, Westphal said. Furthermore, young adults are more likely to develop gambling problems because a human being's central nervous system does not reach full maturity until his or her early twenties, and people younger than 21 exhibit poorer impulse control than older adults, Westphal testified. He therefore concluded that delaying young adults' exposure to the lottery and video poker could reduce the incidence of problem gambling.

Finally, even though Louisiana still allowed 18-year-olds to bet at racetracks and in charitable games, Justice Johnson concluded that a higher age for the lottery and video poker was a rational policy because those forms of gambling were the most popular with young adults.

The legal gambling age elsewhere in the United States varies by state and by form of gambling. In general, the legal age is 21 for casino gaming and 18 for the lottery, pari-mutuel wagering, and charitable gambling such as bingo. In 1999, the National Gambling Impact Study Commission recommended that the legal age be 21 for all forms of gambling in the United States.

their incomes on the lottery. In 1989, Philip Cook and Charles Clotfelder found that people with annual incomes below $10,000 spent more on tickets—$597 per year—than any other income group; that high school dropouts spent four times as much as college graduates; and that African Americans spent five times as much as Caucasians. There is further evidence that lotteries actually help widen the gap between the rich and the poor. In 2005, researchers at the University of Maryland found that lotteries added 10 percent to the increase in the average income gap within a state. In other words, if people with less money grow 20 percent poorer relative to those with more money, the addition of a lottery will aggravate the problem by an additional 2 percent.

Relying on gambling is bad economic policy.

Voting to raise taxes or cut services can have serious political consequences, but legalized gambling has given lawmakers an easy way out of financial troubles. Richard Leone, a member of the NGISC, strongly criticized public officials for this. He wrote:

> Lotteries, especially, seem to bring out the worst in politicians. They are heavily and misleadingly advertised; they pay back to bettors the smallest share of the take of any legal game; and they are an extremely regressive form of taxation, hitting hardest those with least ability to pay. Yet, lotteries have proven to be catnip for elected officials who fear taxation.[94]

Some critics brand the lottery a "quick fix" that addresses a state's immediate financial problems but does little to stabilize government finances in the longer term. Many states have an antiquated tax structure that relies heavily on taxes and fees that fall on working-class and middle-class residents. The influx of lottery revenue allows lawmakers to delay much-needed reform to this system. In any event, gambling revenue makes a smaller contribution to most states' budgets than most people believe. The NGISC found that lotteries contributed only 0.41 to 4.07

Grocery shoppers stop to play some of the slot machines inside an Albertsons grocery store in Las Vegas. Opponents of legalized gambling argue that the increasing accessibility of gambling has had adverse consequences for communities and their economies.

percent of states' general fund revenues. By contrast, sales and income taxes each account for about one-quarter of the average state's general fund revenues. Even in Nevada, gambling revenue represents only 18 percent of the state budget.

One of the leading arguments in favor of the lottery is that it benefits schools. Donald Miller, a professor at St. Mary's College in Indiana, disputes that claim. He found that although states substantially increased per-pupil spending during the first year of the lottery's existence, spending leveled off afterward. In addition to that, per-pupil spending grew more slowly in the long run in lottery states than in non-lottery states. Miller explains:

> The problem is not that lotteries are going belly up. In most states, lottery-generated revenue has continued to grow. But

the politicians couldn't resist using lottery funds to *replace* rather than *add* to existing sources of education funding. Governors and legislators then used money that once had been earmarked for education on tax cuts, new programs or debt reduction—but not for schools.[95]

Promoting economic development is an important function of government. Over the years, federal and state officials

Nevada's Public Policy Toward Gaming

Casino gaming has been legal in Nevada since 1931. Section 463.0129 of the Nevada Revised Statutes sets out the state's public policy concerning gaming:

1. The Legislature hereby finds, and declares to be the public policy of this state, that:
   (a) The gaming industry is vitally important to the economy of the State and the general welfare of the inhabitants.
   (b) The continued growth and success of gaming is dependent upon public confidence and trust that licensed gaming and the manufacture, sale, and distribution of gaming devices and associated equipment are conducted honestly and competitively, that establishments which hold restricted and nonrestricted licenses where gaming is conducted and where gambling devices are operated do not unduly impact the quality of life enjoyed by residents of the surrounding neighborhoods, that the rights of the creditors of licensees are protected and that gaming is free from criminal and corruptive elements.
   (c) Public confidence and trust can only be maintained by strict regulation of all persons, locations, practices, associations, and activities related to the operation of licensed gaming establishments, the manufacture, sale, or distribution of gaming devices and associated equipment, and the operation of inter-casino linked systems.
   (d) All establishments where gaming is conducted and where gaming devices are operated, and manufacturers, sellers, and distributors of

have identified emerging industries and given them financial aid and other incentives to help them prosper. Some believe that the gambling industry is not an appropriate candidate for this kind of assistance. As Goodman points out, "Where we once had government-backed rural electrification, farm irrigation projects, and industrial extension programs, we now get government-backed lotteries, off-track betting, and themed casinos."[96] Unlike alternative energy or biotechnology, gambling is a "zero-sum"

certain gaming devices and equipment, and operators of inter-casino linked systems must therefore be licensed, controlled and assisted to protect the public health, safety, morals, good order, and general welfare of the inhabitants of the State, to foster the stability and success of gaming and to preserve the competitive economy and policies of free competition of the State of Nevada.

(e) To ensure that gaming is conducted honestly, competitively, and free of criminal and corruptive elements, all gaming establishments in this state must remain open to the general public and the access of the general public to gaming activities must not be restricted in any manner except as provided by the Legislature.

2. No applicant for a license or other affirmative commission approval has any right to a license or the granting of the approval sought. Any license issued or other commission approval granted pursuant to the provisions of this chapter or chapter 464 [which governs pari-mutuel wagering] is a revocable privilege, and no holder acquires any vested right therein or thereunder.

3. This section does not:

(a) Abrogate or abridge any common-law right of a gaming establishment to exclude any person from gaming activities or eject any person from the premises of the establishment for any reason; or

(b) Prohibit a licensee from establishing minimum wagers for any gambling game or slot machine.

industry that merely recirculates money—frequently, into the hands of shareholders and executives of gambling companies—and creates no added wealth.

Goodman believes that the rush to embrace gambling will eventually be seen as a serious blunder on the part of U.S. public officials:

> Choosing to bet on America's luck business represents another case of governments resorting to a magic-bullet cure for their economic woes. For more than 40 years, such simplistic approaches have been tried again and again. In the 1950s and 1960s, it was called "urban renewal"—cities were torn to shreds to eliminate slums and attract more business and more affluent residents. During the 1970s and 1980s, it became a game known as "industrial recruitment" or "smokestack chasing"—local and state governments pitted themselves against one another in an effort to woo companies with tax breaks, subsidies, and promises of low wages and lax environmental standards.[97]

Betting the future on gambling sends citizens the wrong message, Goodman adds. He accuses public officials of "encouraging a public perception that governments can do little to support a healthier economic climate for all citizens, and that the best they can do is to provide enormous windfalls for those fortunate enough to work for these companies."[98]

Summary

When lotteries were relegalized, they were placed under state control in order to avoid the abuses of the past. These state-run lotteries have nevertheless failed to serve the public interest. They offer worse odds than other forms of legalized gambling, and lottery advertising misleads people about their chances of winning and where the revenue goes. The widespread availability of tickets encourages the poor, heavy players, and young people to buy tickets. Lawmakers have portrayed the lottery and other forms of gambling as a solution to state fiscal problems; however, gambling revenue makes only a modest contribution to state finances and does little to promote the long-term health of the economy.

Government Policy Has Made Gaming Less Harmful

Two actions in Renaissance Italy paved the way for today's government-regulated gambling. The first involved the lottery, which was originally run by merchants:

City authorities or the local nobles soon demanded a measure of consumer protection, attention to public welfare, and a piece of the action: They insisted that all drawings be rigorously inspected to ensure their honesty and that a portion of the profits go to either the needy poor or the authorities themselves. With this transformation, the modern lottery was born, as here can be found two key elements of today's government-sanctioned lotteries—a supervisory commission and the redistribution of revenues for charitable purposes.[99]

The second governmental action was the opening of casino gaming. In 1638, Venice's Great Council opened Europe's first legal, state-sanctioned public gaming house. "The opening of the

Ridotto represented a historic union between mercantile gamblers, who ran games for profit, and government, who sought to legitimize the gamblers for purposes of public order and revenue enhancement."[100] The Ridotto was the forerunner of today's casinos, which operate under government supervision in dozens of countries around the world.

Government successfully regulates other "vices."

Society chooses to regulate, rather than ban outright, some dangerous products and activities. Prohibition of alcohol is the best-known example to happen in the United States. Between 1920 and 1933, it was illegal in all states to buy alcoholic beverages. Prohibition did not stop Americans from drinking, nor did it put an end to problems such as drunk driving and domestic violence. Prohibition also dismantled the controls that had previously existed, making alcohol even more of a menace. The staff of *Consumer Reports* magazine described what happened:

Instead of consuming alcoholic beverages manufactured under the safeguards of state and federal standards, for example, people now drank "rotgut," some of it adulterated, some of it contaminated. The use of methyl alcohol, a poison, because ethyl alcohol was unavailable or too costly, led to blindness and death; "ginger jake," an adulterant found in bootleg beverages, produced paralysis and death. The disreputable saloon was replaced by the even less savory speakeasy. . . . There were legal closing hours for saloons; the speakeasies stayed open night and day. Organized crime syndicates took control of alcohol distribution.[101]

Even though the 1920s opened eyes to alcohol's destructive potential, officials nevertheless voted to repeal Prohibition because they concluded that the alternative was worse. However, when states relegalized alcohol, they imposed stricter controls than those of pre-Prohibition days. For example, manufacturers could not sell their products directly to the public; retail sellers had to be licensed. A wide range of business practices were regulated, from when alcohol could be sold to how it could be advertised. An age limit was put in place, too, with those under a certain age, usually 21, prohibited from buying. Regulation has not eliminated alcohol abuse, but most Americans believe that the current approach is better than outright prohibition. The United States also follows much the same regulatory approach with respect to guns and tobacco products: There are restrictions on where they can be sold and by whom, and to whom.

Lottery Advertising Guidelines

In 1975, Congress relaxed the federal government's long-standing opposition to lotteries and passed a law permitting newspapers and broadcasters to advertise lotteries in states where they were legal. As a result of that legislation and Supreme Court decisions limiting the government's power to restrict commercial speech, states now spend hundreds of millions of dollars to advertise their lotteries.

Promoters of legal gambling have been criticized for encouraging irresponsible and underage play, and states with lotteries are no exception. In 1999, the North American Association of State and Provincial Lotteries responded to critics by adopting a set of voluntary advertising standards.* The association generally recommended that advertising be tasteful, not portray excessive or abusive gambling or illegal activity, not encourage players to bet beyond their means, and not portray the lottery as a solution to a player's financial problems. It also urged that advertising encourage bettors to play responsibly.

The association further recommend that advertising emphasize the entertainment value of playing, not portray the lottery as an investment or an alternative to working, and not overstate the chances of winning. It also recommended that the odds of winning be clearly disclosed to players and that the public be clearly told where lottery proceeds go.

With respect to underage play, the association recommended that the age restriction be posted where tickets are sold, that advertisements not portray actors who are underage or who appear to be underage, and that promotions not be aimed at those who are too young to buy tickets.

* North American Association of State and Provincial Lotteries, "NASPL Advertising Guidelines," available online, http://www.naspl.org/index.cfm?fuseaction=content&PageID=39.

Before casinos spread beyond Nevada, many states had successfully regulated pari-mutuel wagering, which was once the most popular form of gaming. A century ago, antigambling forces prevailed upon lawmakers in all but a handful of states to outlaw betting on horse races. David Schwartz explains how the industry responded: "Pressed to the wall by antigambling reformers, horse advocates began to put their house in order. In addition to eliminating the need for bookmakers, they instituted drug testing and used technology, including improved starting gates and photo-finish cameras, to make races fairer."[102]

When states relegalized wagering, they also comprehensively regulated the racing industry. Those regulations exist to this day. Horse owners, jockeys, and racetrack personnel must be licensed, and state racing commissions can deny a license for a variety of reasons, ranging from a criminal conviction to making false statements to regulators. Because racing is so thoroughly regulated, fixed races are believed to be rare.

The gaming industry is closely regulated.

Many Americans still associate gaming with organized crime. The American Gaming Association (AGA) blames this perception in part on films such as *Bugsy* and *Casino*, which are fictional accounts of a Las Vegas that existed years ago. Nevada long ago took steps to rid the gaming industry of organized criminals. In 1959, the state created the Nevada Gaming Control Commission, which is in charge of issuing licenses and regulating the gaming industry. Nevada requires a wide variety of individuals and businesses to be licensed. Manufacturers of gaming devices, owners of real estate underneath casinos, and lenders to gaming companies, for example, must be licensed, along with the casinos themselves.

Nevada has also repealed antiquated laws that forced casinos to rely on unconventional sources of income such as union pension funds. David Schwarz explains:

In 1967 and 1969, thanks to the advocacy of Governor Paul Laxalt, the legislature amended the gaming laws to permit full-fledged corporate ownership of gaming properties. Publicly traded corporations were permitted to enter the gaming business, provided that they adhered to strict licensing guidelines: All shareholders, directors, and officers of the corporate subsidiary that directly ran the casino had to be licensed.[103]

When states outside Nevada legalized casinos, they, too, legislated strict oversight of the gaming industry. If anything, those states were even stricter than Nevada because they followed the "New Jersey model," which assumes that gaming is potentially dangerous but capable of producing benefits if regulated carefully. When first enacted, New Jersey's regulations were so thorough

Improving Casino Regulation

The National Gambling Impact Study Commission offered several proposals for "best practices" in the gaming industry. Michael Belletire, the former chairman of the Illinois Gaming Board, offered one proposal that dealt with casino regulation. Since 1976, 10 states have joined Nevada in legalizing commercial casinos and, in a number of other states, Native American tribes have agreed to give state gaming regulators the authority to oversee their operations.

The independence and honesty of state regulators is a fundamental concern, Belletire said. That concern exists because, in an effort to prevent casinos from proliferating, most states limit the number of casino licenses that can be issued. The fewer licenses, the more valuable they are—a situation that, some believe, invites corruption. In Louisiana, more than $3 million in bribes were paid in exchange for licenses, and that state's ex-governor was sent to prison for a number of crimes relating to gaming. (When Mississippi legalized casinos, it tried to avoid Louisiana's experience by leaving it up to market forces rather than state regulators to determine how many casinos the state could support.)

According to Belletire, that regulatory power should be given to an appointed independent body rather than a single individual who might be subject to that they even dictated what color felt could be used on gaming tables. Strict state regulation, combined with federal laws aimed at organized crime, made it more difficult for underworld figures to infiltrate the gaming industry. By 1999, the National Gambling Impact Study Commission (NGISC) was able to say: "All of the evidence presented to the Commission indicates that effective state regulation, coupled with the takeover of much of the industry by public corporations, has eliminated organized crime from the direct ownership and operation of casinos."[104]

According to the AGA, commercial casinos are one of the nation's most thoroughly regulated industries:

> Funded by tax dollars from gaming, a large work force of
> regulators in each state monitors industry activities. Nevada

political influence. He also suggested that the regulatory body's decision be open to appeal to some higher authority to ensure that it acts properly.

Belletire proposed a number of measures aimed at curbing inappropriate influence over the process of awarding licenses. He proposed that states draw up clear standards for deciding which applicants are given licenses, receive competitive proposals from applicants for licenses, and insist that applicants fully disclose their financial and political relationships. Belletire also recommended that the regulatory body have broad power to examine the background and integrity of owners and key persons in casino companies. He specifically recommended that regulators exclude convicted felons from the gaming industry, and also require casino companies to disassociate themselves from "unsuitable" individuals. In addition, he recommended that regulators stop casino companies from doing business with outside vendors that have unsuitable key personnel.

With respect to day-to-day enforcement, Belletire called video surveillance "one of the most powerful tools" in overseeing casino operations. He recommended that casino operators be held accountable for "failing to consistently and diligently deter and detect attempts" by underage players to enter casinos or place bets. He also called on states to make underage gambling a misdemeanor-level offense and to allow casinos to bring criminal charges against cheaters.

alone employs 432 regulators at a cost of nearly $30.8 million, while New Jersey employs 714 regulators at a cost of $62.7 million. . . . The total cost of regulation in fiscal year 2002 in the 11 commercial states was more than $202 million, with 2,455 regulators and support staff helping to ensure that only legitimate interests are involved in this business.[105]

The same is true of Native American–run gaming. The National Indian Gaming Commission (NIGC) points out that tribal gaming operations are regulated at three distinct levels: the Indian nations themselves; state gaming commissions; and federal agencies, including the NIGC and the Justice, Treasury, and Interior departments. The NIGC reports that tribal governments have adopted the same standards as the commercial casino industry, and "as a result of this three tier system, Indian gaming is subject to more stringent regulation and security controls than any other type of gaming in the United States."[106]

The gaming industry's self-regulation complements government regulation.

Casinos know that if they employ undesirables or market themselves to underage or pathological gamblers, the resulting bad publicity would cost them business. Worse still, it could lead to harsher regulations. As a result, the gaming industry has adopted a comprehensive set of measures under which companies police themselves. In 2003, the AGA adopted voluntary standards[107] that are intended "to make responsible gaming an integral part of our daily operations across the United States."[108] The guidelines cover practices ranging from advertising to the serving of alcohol. In particular, they set out measures for curbing underage and pathological gambling and encouraging those with problems to get help. In addition, the gaming industry has contributed more than $15 million to the National Center for Responsible Gaming (NCRG), and has also contributed to the

Institute for Research on Pathological Gambling and Related Disorders at Harvard Medical School.

Lotteries also regulate themselves. In 1999, the North American Association of State and Provincial Lotteries (NASPL) adopted a set of guidelines[109] that govern lottery advertising. The objective of those guidelines is to encourage adults to make responsible decisions when playing the lottery. The NASPL notes that there is another check on advertising: "Remember, too, that lottery advertising is seen by lottery critics as well as lottery players. If an ad is seen as even marginally objectionable, these critics do not hesitate to make their opinions known in the political arena."[110]

Because lotteries are operated by the states, they are accountable to the public. The NASPL explains:

> State regulatory proceedings are much more open and accessible to the public than the workings of federal regulatory agencies. All lottery board meetings are public, as are all legislative hearings. Lottery files are public records, subject at any time to media scrutiny. Lottery opponents in a legislature can examine the smallest lottery details and vote on lottery business operations.[111]

Public opinion discourages lottery officials from engaging in abusive marketing practices or lying to the public about how the lottery is run. Furthermore, citizens have the ultimate check on lottery officials: They can stop buying tickets.

Legal gaming is more honest.

It is in the public interest for gaming to take place in the open rather than underground. As Wharton School Professor Justin Wolfers observed, "Bettors value regulation: They get paid, their legs don't get broken, and they can talk about their wagers around the water cooler with no legal risk."[112]

As pointed out earlier, the fact that sports betting is legal in Nevada discourages cheating because legal bookmakers have an economic incentive to alert the authorities to fixed games without the fear of being prosecuted. Even the NCAA, despite its strong objections to betting on college games, has worked with a Las Vegas–based firm that develops betting lines in order to learn about attempts to fix games.

Wolfers also argues that legalizing gaming can bring gaming-related problems into the open where they can be dealt with:

> The competitive advantage conferred by regulation may also channel problem gamblers into the legal sector. If policymakers build in sufficient safeguards, we can direct victims of compulsive gambling into treatment. Instead, today's problem gamblers are channeled by illegal bookmakers into ever-higher losses, and their mounting financial pressures sometimes lead to criminal conduct.[113]

Even "looking the other way" at illegal gaming might be preferable to prohibiting it. During the Klondike gold rush at the end of the nineteenth century, gaming was widespread in saloons in the boomtown of Dawson. Even though Canadian law barred such gaming, the North West Mounted Police allowed it to go on in public anyway. David Schwartz explains why: "Superintendent Charles Constantine freely stated in the late 1890s that he would not restrict gambling. He rationalized that, out in the open, gamblers would be forced to run a 'square game,' while if driven underground they would resort to cheating. Since the miners would gamble anyway, it was best to give them some measure of protection."[114]

The lottery is a benign form of gaming.

State-run lotteries are the most popular form of legalized gaming in the United States. A 2006 Pew survey found that a majority of adults had bought a lottery ticket during the past year.

For a variety of reasons, the lottery is less conducive to problem gambling than other forms of gaming. To begin with, the price of a typical ticket is $1, which does not lend itself to high-stakes betting. In 1997, each American adult spent an average of $150 on lottery tickets. Even when those who do not buy tickets are factored out, the average lottery player still spends about $300 per year—less than a dollar a day. The NASPL offers more reasons why the lottery does not attract problem gamblers:

> [Other kinds of gaming provide] a sense of high excitement, usually involving considerable sensory stimulation. Lottery tickets do not provide this. A second factor is a sense of mastery or skill. Lotteries have no skill element. A third is the immediacy of the result and reward and the ability to play repeatedly and quickly. Numbers game drawings typically take place some time after the purchase is made, and players have to wait between a day and a week to play again, making chasing losses difficult. . . . It's quite different from pulling the slot machine handle and watching the coins come out.[115]

According to the NASPL, only 4 percent of the calls to Minnesota's hotline for problem gambling and only 6 percent of the calls to Iowa's hotline were related to the lottery. In addition, a study of 944 people who checked into Minnesota's gambling treatment centers between 1990 and 1996 found that only 8 had named the lottery as their preferred form of gambling.

The NASPL also argues against the often-heard criticism that lotteries target the poor. The association cites Gallup's Gambling in America survey, which found that people with incomes of $45,000 to $75,000 were the most likely to play and those with incomes under $25,000 were the least likely. That survey also found that players with incomes higher than $75,000 spent three times as much on tickets as those with incomes under $25,000. In any event, the association points out: "It's a bad business decision to target marketing to a small portion of the population with the least disposable income and who are the least likely to buy the product. It's a bad political decision as such a practice is almost certain to earn a lottery the wrath of the governor, the legislature, and the media."[116]

Finally, the NASPL also maintains that lottery advertising uses up slightly more than 1 percent of total revenue, a considerably

The American Gaming Association's Code of Conduct

In 2003, the American Gaming Association (AGA), the casino industry's trade group, adopted a "Code of Conduct for Responsible Gaming."* It is a set of recommended "best practices" for casinos to follow.

In the "Pledge to Our Employees," casinos commit themselves to educate employees about responsible gaming and tell them where they can find help if they have a gambling problem.

In the "Pledge to Our Patrons" casinos commit themselves to put out brochures for players that encourage responsible gambling, provide a toll-free number for a problem gambling help line, and provide information that explains the odds of winning. In addition, casinos will allow customers to opt out of promotional mailing campaigns, exclude themselves from taking advantage of on-site check cashing or short-term loans, and even exclude themselves from the casinos altogether.

With respect to underage gambling, casinos pledge to keep underage people out of the gaming area, post signs reminding players of the legal gambling age, and train employees to deal with underage betting, underage smoking and drinking, and unattended children left in gaming areas by their parents.

With respect to serving alcoholic beverages, casinos pledge to enforce the legal drinking age, not serve visibly intoxicated patrons, and stop visibly intoxicated players from continuing to gamble.

Finally, casinos pledge to advertise responsibly. In general, advertising should reflect "generally accepted contemporary standards of good taste," strictly comply with all state and federal standards, and not make false or misleading claims. In addition, casino advertising and marketing materials should not do any of the following:

smaller percentage than what restaurant owners, beverage companies, or candy makers spend to promote their products. In addition, the association denies that lotteries target heavy players. It points out that no matter what the product, some people are more enthusiastic consumers than others and, as a result, about 20 percent of the population will account for 80 percent of that product's sales.

- Contain cartoon figures, symbols, celebrity or entertainer endorsements, or language designed to appeal to underage gamblers

- Feature current college athletes

- Feature anyone who is or appears to be below the legal gambling age

- Claim that gaming will guarantee an individual's social, financial, or personal success

- Be placed in media specifically oriented to young people or where most of the audience is reasonably expected to be too young to legally gamble

- Imply or suggest any illegal activity

- Appear next to or near comics or other material that appeals to young people

- Be placed at any venue where most of the audience is normally expected to be underage

Finally, in the "Pledge to the Public," the gaming industry commits itself to fund the National Center for Responsible Gaming, use the center's research to identify best practices for the promotion of responsible gaming, and "continue to develop a dialogue" surrounding scientific research on gambling and health. It also calls on every casino company to conduct an annual review of its compliance with the code of conduct.

* American Gaming Association, "Code of Conduct for Responsible Gaming," Responsible Gaming, available online, http://www.americangaming.org/programs/responsible gaming/code_public.cfm.

Summary

One lesson that Americans learned from Prohibition is that banning a so-called vice also eliminated laws that regulated it. For that reason, society has concluded that regulating gaming is a wiser policy than trying to legislate it out of existence. Regulation makes it more likely that organized criminals are kept out of the business. It also reduces the likelihood that bettors will be cheated and, in the case of sports betting, makes sure that the games themselves are honest and fair. The gaming industry also regulates itself in an effort to avoid both bad publicity and tighter legal restrictions. The lottery, which is not only state regulated but state run, is a benign form of gaming because stakes are relatively low and traditional lottery games offer little of the stimulation that attracts problem gamblers.

The Future of Legalized Gambling

In 1999, the National Gambling Impact Study Commission (NGISC) described the nature of today's gaming landscape: "Once exotic, gambling has quickly taken its place in mainstream culture: Televised megabucks drawings; senior citizens' day-trips to nearby casinos; and the transformation of Las Vegas into family friendly theme resorts, in which gambling is but one of a menu of attractions, have become familiar backdrops to daily life."[117]

Just how popular has gambling become? David Schwartz observed: "It is too early to judge the bigger sweep of history, but it seems that the world is entering a sustained period of gambling's growth not seen since the European gambling boom of 1650–1800."[118] A 2006 Pew survey bears this out. It found that two-thirds of Americans had gambled within the past year;

52 percent of them had bought a lottery ticket, 29 percent went to a casino, and 24 percent played slot machines.

The Impact of the Gambling Commission

The NGISC took a middle ground with respect to legalized gambling. Its key recommendation was a pause on the expansion of gambling until public officials learned more about its effects. The commission called for a rollback of only convenience gambling and betting on amateur and college sports. It also found that Native American–run gaming had helped some tribes and that "destination" casinos could benefit poor communities.

The NGISC recommended that states raise the legal age to 21 for all forms of gambling. In addition, it urged tougher enforcement of gaming laws, especially with respect to underage play, and for an end of promotional campaigns that targeted the poor. The commission called for federally sponsored studies of pathological and problem gambling, and encouraged states to regularly review the extent of the problem.

Not everyone was satisfied with the NGISC's work. Opponents of legalized gambling complained that it was too willing to accept commercial and tribal casinos and continued state operation of lotteries. On the other hand, some criticized the commission for having overemphasized the negative effects of legalized gambling. Robert Loescher, a member of the commission, said the following: "The overall report is weighted heavily to a small percentage of the American public that are burdened with very real problem and pathological gambling. The report does little to acknowledge the fact that millions of Americans participate in and enjoy gaming as entertainment without any problems."[119]

Despite the NGISC's call for a pause, Americans gamble more than ever. Gaming revenue totaled $58.2 billion in 1999, the year the commission released its report, and rose to $83.7 billion in 2005. The main reason for the increase is the continued spread of tribal casinos, whose revenues more than tripled between 1995 and 2005. In 2000, California voters authorized blackjack and slot machines on tribal lands. Today, that state's tribal gaming operations take in more revenue than all the casinos on the Las Vegas strip combined. Meanwhile, key recommendations by the commission have gone unheeded. Nevada bookmakers still take bets on college games, there has been no rollback of convenience gambling, and people younger than 21 are allowed to take part in some forms of gambling.

Will Gaming Remain Legal?

The American people appear to accept legalized gambling in principle. The NGISC found: "Although some communities may decide to restrict or even ban existing gambling, there is not much prospect of its being outlawed altogether. It is clear that the American people want legalized gambling and it has already sunk deep economic and other roots in many communities."[120] In 2006, a Gallup survey found that 60 percent of Americans considered gambling morally acceptable, compared to 34 percent who consider it morally unacceptable. That same year, another survey commissioned by the AGA found that 50 percent of Americans considered casino gaming acceptable for everyone, and only 18 percent considered it unacceptable for everyone. Also in 2006, a Pew survey found that 71 percent of Americans approved of lotteries, 66 percent approved of bingo, and 51 percent approved of casino gaming.

At the same time, the NGISC noted, a substantial number of Americans have misgivings about at least some forms of legalized gambling: "Opponents can include those opposed to all gambling, those content with the current extent of gambling but opposed to its expansion, those favoring one type of gambling but opposed to another, and those who simply want to keep gambling out of their particular community, the latter being less motivated by questions of probity than of zoning."[121] A 2006

The National Gambling Impact Study Commission Report

In 1976, the Commission on the Review of the National Policy Toward Gambling released a report entitled *Gambling in America*. In the years that followed, legalized gambling increased substantially in the United States. Critics argued that federal and state officials had acted too quickly to legalize gambling, and called for another federal study. Congress responded to those calls by passing the National Gambling Impact Study Commission Act of 1996 (Public Law 104-169), which created a nine-member commission to study gambling's economic and social impact.

In 1999, the commission released its report.* Its main recommendation was that no new forms of gambling be authorized until public officials find out more about the economic and social benefits and costs of existing forms of gambling. The commission's specific recommendations included the following:

- Except for tribal and Internet gaming, states are best equipped to regulate gambling.

- The legal gambling age should be 21, and the age limit should be strictly enforced. Students should be warned of the dangers of gambling, beginning at the elementary level and continuing through college.

- Gambling facilities should warn players about the risks of gambling, and post the odds of winning when feasible.

- Lawmakers should impose stringent controls on the gaming industry's contributions to political campaigns.

- Betting on college and amateur sports should be banned altogether. In addition, government and the private sector should warn the public that sports betting could have serious consequences.

- Government should ban aggressive advertising, especially advertising that targets young people and the poor.

- States should not authorize casino-type games at racetracks ("racinos").

- The gaming industry should adopt advertising guidelines.

- Congress should bring state lotteries and tribal gaming under federal truth-in-advertising laws.

- Gambling regulators should be barred from working in the gaming industry for one year after leaving the government.

- Units of government should periodically reassess the effects of those forms of gambling that are legal in order to determine which forms should be expanded, limited, or abolished. Before legalizing new forms of gambling or expanding existing ones, the government should analyze their economic and social effects.

- Lottery states should reduce their dependence on low-income and heavy bettors, for example, by reducing the number of sales outlets in certain areas.

- States should require licensees to adopt an anti–problem gambling and anti–pathological gambling program that includes training employees on how to recognize bettors with serious gambling problems.

- States should levy a "privilege tax" on gaming companies. The tax money would fund efforts to prevent and treat problem gambling.

- Health insurers should be required by law to cover treatment for gambling problems.

- Gaming facilities should be required by law to adopt "self-exclusion" programs under which a problem gambler can ask to be banned from entering.

- Congress should not allow Internet gambling beyond that which is already legal in the United States. It should ban wire transfers to known gambling Web sites, and also bar credit card issuers from collecting debts from players who had lost money gambling online.

- States should not allow the expansion of gambling into peoples' homes.

- The United States should discourage foreign governments from harboring Web sites that target American bettors.

(continues)

(continued)
- Cash advance machines should be banned from the immediate area where gambling takes place.

- Casino development should be targeted for communities with high levels of unemployment. The emphasis should be on "destination-style" casinos, which create more and better jobs.

* National Gambling Impact and Policy Commission, *The National Gambling Impact Study Commission: final report* (Washington, DC: The Commission, 1999).

Pew survey found that 54 percent of Americans opposed legalizing sports betting. That same year, a Harris survey found that 53 percent opposed legalizing online gambling.

In the near future, debate will focus on whether to expand existing forms of gambling and whether to legalize new ones. Robert Goodman believes that the pendulum will eventually swing away from legalization:

> As more and more people experience gambling within their own communities, its costly problems will become more evident. This has happened before in our history. The current gambling boom has obvious parallels with the one which occurred in nineteenth-century America, when gambling ventures proliferated until corruption and abuses produced federal legislation outlawing all forms of gambling in the 1890s.[122]

Professor I. Nelson Rose agrees. He maintains that the United States has seen three "waves" of widespread public gambling, each of which was followed by public backlash and prohibition. In 1991, Rose predicted that gaming would be illegal within 40 years.

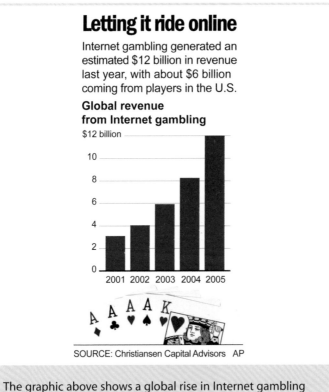

Letting it ride online

Internet gambling generated an estimated $12 billion in revenue last year, with about $6 billion coming from players in the U.S.

Global revenue from Internet gambling

SOURCE: Christiansen Capital Advisors AP

The graphic above shows a global rise in Internet gambling as measured by the revenue it generated from 2001 to 2006. Online gambling is not subject to the same restrictions as its more conventional forms.

Even though gambling prohibition is unlikely, the industry might be facing a problem with saturation. In 2007, the authors of a status report on gambling observed: "Industry analysts believe that many sectors of the American gambling market are reaching maturity. In other words, the growth spurt of the past few decades is likely over. Commercial casino gambling has not spread beyond the 11 states in which it operated in 1996."[123] In 2005, Americans wagered more in casinos in their home states than out of state, suggesting that the casino industry is running out of new markets. Some observers add that the lottery is suffering from "jackpot fatigue"—meaning players have gotten used to huge payouts—and the public is growing bored with existing games. Horse racing has been in decline for years, in spite of simulcasts and off-track betting. In some states, racetracks survive only because they have added slot machines and become racinos.

Should the Federal Government Regulate Gambling?

In 1976 and again in 1999, federal commissions recommended that states take primary responsibility for controlling gambling. This stance is consistent with the U.S. constitutional system under which the federal government exercises regulatory power in carefully spelled-out areas, such as the armed forces and the postal service, while state and local governments have the power to promote the public health, safety, and welfare.

Two developments have heightened the federal role in regulating gambling. The first (discussed later in this chapter) is the rise of Internet-based gambling. The second is tribal gaming. The Supreme Court's decision in 1987 in *California v. Cabazon Band of Mission Indians* led Congress to pass the Indian Gaming Regulatory Act (IGRA), which provides a framework for the regulation of tribal gaming. Critics of IGRA, including some state officials, argue that the law puts undue pressure on states to approve tribal gaming, including forms of gambling that state residents do not want. Some also accuse the federal government of promoting gaming in order to avoid spending on the tribes. In 1999, Supreme Court Justice John Paul Stevens observed that because of the government's pro–tribal gaming stance, "the federal policy of discouraging gambling in general, and casino gambling in particular, is now decidedly equivocal."[124]

Some observers believe that the federal government should step in and reverse the "race to the bottom" that causes gambling to spread from one state to another. Robert Goodman argues:

> Left to their own devices, states and cities have few options but to compete with adjacent governments in using gambling ventures to attract one another's residents. Many local politicians, even those who oppose expansion, find themselves favoring casino development simply as a defensive measure to keep state residents from betting in neighboring cities, states, or nearby Indian reservations. Federal oversight and coordination of gambling development can help prevent this kind of competitive scramble among neighboring jurisdictions.[125]

While he was in the U.S. Senate, Paul Simon offered two proposals aimed at reducing the financial pressure on states to legalize gambling. The first was a 5 percent tax on the gross revenues of *future* legalized gambling, which would defray some of the social costs of gambling and slow down the trend toward market saturation. The other was a subsidy to those states and Indian tribes that opted not to allow gambling.

Should Sports Betting Be Legalized?

The Professional and Amateur Sports Protection Act of 1992[126] outlawed the spread of sports betting beyond the handful of states where some form of wagering was already legal. The act effectively limited legal sports betting to licensed bookmakers in Nevada. In spite of the law, betting on sports is one of the most popular forms of gambling. Those who want to end the ban argue that legalizing and regulating sports betting would drive organized crime out of bookmaking, as was the case with casino regulation. They also maintain that legal bookmakers have helped the authorities find and punish those who have fixed games. William A. Bible, the former chairman of the Nevada Gaming Control Board, argued:

Not one college sports scandal is the result of legal sports wagering. To the contrary, legal sports wagering in Nevada has assisted athletic leagues in their enforcement activities aimed at preventing game fixing and point shaving. Instead of further restricting legal sports wagering, the Commission would have been better served to recognize sports wagering's overwhelming participatory acceptance by the American people and to recommend, instead, further legalization and strict regulation.[127]

Gambling-Related Legislation in the 110th Congress

The Unlawful Internet Gambling Enforcement Act of 2006 (UIGEA) was the first major federal law that addressed online gambling. A number of bills dealing with online gambling in particular and gambling in general were under consideration by the 110th Congress, which began work in January 2007. Those bills include the following:

H.R. 1170, the Comprehensive Awareness of Problem Gambling Act of 2007. This bill would address problem gambling by authorizing a national media campaign to raise public awareness, creating a national research program, and providing governmental agencies and non-profit organizations with grants to operate prevention and treatment programs. It would also express the sense of Congress that states should devote a percentage of their gambling revenue to prevention and treatment.

H.R. 2046, the Internet Gambling Regulation and Enforcement Act of 2007. This bill would lift the federal ban on certain forms of online gambling and provide instead for its licensing and regulation. The federal Financial Crimes Enforcement Network, a division of the Treasury Department, would be placed in charge of licensing. States and Native American tribes could "opt out" and either prohibit online gambling altogether or

Opponents are concerned that legalizing sports betting would increase the frequency of game fixing. The NCAA is especially concerned. It points out that student-athletes are not paid for playing college sports and thus more vulnerable to offers of cash to fix games—especially if they are already in debt as the result of gambling. The at-risk population appears to be large. According to a survey conducted on behalf of the NCAA in 2004, 35 percent of male athletes said that they had placed a bet on some sporting event, and 21 percent said that they had bet on a college game.

restrict it to certain forms of gambling. In addition, professional sports leagues and the governing bodies of college and amateur sports could prohibit online betting on their games.

H.R. 2140, the Internet Gambling Study Act. This bill is aimed at carrying out a recommendation of the National Gambling Impact Study Commission. It would authorize a wide-ranging study of online gambling by the National Research Council of the National Academy of Sciences. The study would include the extent of online gambling and its impact on young people and compulsive gamblers; its legal status, both in the United States and abroad; the effectiveness of UIGEA and other federal laws; the extent to which terrorists and organized crime groups are exploiting online gambling; the experience of other countries that permit online gambling; and the potential tax revenue that would result from legalizing it in the United States.

H.R. 2610, the Skill Game Protection Act. This bill would lift the federal ban on online games such as poker, chess, and bridge in which success is predominantly determined by a player's skill and the site operator is not a participant in the game. It would be up to the states to decide whether to allow their residents to play games of skill online. It would direct the secretary of the U.S. Treasury to adopt regulations aimed at curbing fraud, money laundering, participation by underage and compulsive gamblers, and violations of players' privacy. This bill would also make clear that the Wire Act applies only to sports betting.

It has been argued that gambling cheapens sports. According to Senator Bill Bradley, a former professional athlete:

> State-sanctioned sports betting conveys the message that sports are more about money than personal achievement and sportsmanship. In these days of scandal and disillusionment, it is important that our youngsters not receive this message . . . sports betting threatens the integrity of and public confidence in professional and amateur team sports, converting sports from wholesome athletic entertainment into a vehicle for gambling . . . sports gambling raises people's suspicions about point-shaving and game-fixing. All of this puts undue pressure on players, coaches, and officials.[128]

Congress took up legislation that would have banned all betting on amateur sports but did not pass it. A bill in the current Congress would lift the federal ban on sports betting, but it is not considered likely to pass.

Is it Possible to Regulate Online Gambling?

Internet gaming arrived so recently that scientists have compiled little data about its effects. Opponents offer a number of reasons for banning it. The primary reason involves young people: teenagers and college students are the heaviest users of the Internet, and it is difficult to enforce age limits online. The NGISC warned, "While 'know your customer' is a motto of the gambling industry, this becomes particularly challenging through technologies available to Internet users. Screening clients to determine age or if they have a history of gambling problems is difficult at best."[129]

There are other objections to online gaming: Online gamblers tend to play alone, and scientists have found a link between solitary gambling and pathological gambling. Web sites also provide an opportunity for money laundering, the transfer of ill-gotten money through third parties in order to hide its origins. Drug dealers, for instance, could deliberately lose their money to an online casino that is part of the same crime organization. Finally, offshore casinos operate under much looser regulation than land-based casinos in the United States, leaving Americans with no legal recourse if they are cheated or the casino operator disappears with their money.

Federal officials oppose legalization. In their fight against online casinos and sports books, they continue to rely on the Interstate Wire Act of 1961 (Wire Act), a law that was passed long before the Internet came into existence. They do so because Congress has not modernized the Wire Act or even made clear what it applies to. During the late 1990s, Congress considered, but failed to pass, legislation that would have heavily restricted online gambling.

In 2006, Congress passed the Unlawful Internet Gambling Enforcement Act (UIGEA). The law was intended to discourage online gambling by barring the transfer of funds from American bettors to online gambling sites. Some observers think that the UIGEA is merely symbolic and that serious gamblers will find a way to place bets online. The authors of a status report on gambling observed, "Many people believe that those determined to gamble online will find a way, probably by going to foreign, private payment processors and casinos."[130] Nevertheless, after UIGEA passed, the 10 largest online gambling sites reported that they had lost more than half their business.

At first, the gaming industry favored a ban on online gaming. It has since changed its position. The AGA states that it would support Internet gambling legislation if it were to meet three tests: "1) The right of states to regulate gaming must be protected. 2) It must not create competitive advantages or disadvantages between and among commercial casinos, Native

American casinos, state lotteries, and pari-mutuel wagering operations; and 3) No form of gaming that currently is legal should be made illegal."[131] Legislation that would license and regulate online gambling operators has been introduced in Congress, but it is not considered likely to pass.

Many believe that technology and the globalization of the world economy make it difficult for the U.S. government to regulate gambling, let alone put a stop to it. Richard Hoffer believes that the U.S. government will eventually give up on prohibiting gaming:

> There will come a day, sooner rather than later, when the case for prohibition is exhausted and the U.S. lawmakers simply give up. The one thing we know, prohibition doesn't work so well in this country; we like to do what we like to do. It might be that the Wire Act will simply become one of those legal curiosities, like a law against spitting on the sidewalk. It'll just pass away. That's sort of what's happening right now; the sports books continue to operate, with less and less formal opposition, until it just becomes the norm.[132]

Summary

Gambling, in some form or other, is legal in most of the United States. Americans agree in principle with legalized gambling, but favor keeping online gambling illegal and oppose sports betting. The National Gambling Impact Study Commission took a middle ground in the controversy. Its main recommendation was that public officials delay the expansion of legalized gambling until they learn more about its effects on society. The commission called for a rollback of convenience gambling, a ban on betting on amateur sports, and a minimum age of 21 for all gambling. By and large, those recommendations have not become law. Sports betting remains illegal outside Nevada, and is likely to remain so. The federal government opposes the legalization of online gaming, and has tried to prosecute opera-tors of gambling Web sites. But enforcement is difficult, and some observers believe that efforts to stop online gambling will ultimately fail.

Beginning Legal Research

The goals of each book in the POINT-COUNTERPOINT series are not only to give the reader a basic introduction to a controversial issue affecting society, but also to encourage the reader to explore the issue more fully. This Appendix is meant to serve as a guide to the reader in researching the current state of the law as well as exploring some of the public policy arguments as to why existing laws should be changed or new laws are needed.

Although some sources of law can be found primarily in law libraries, legal research has become much faster and more accessible with the advent of the Internet. This Appendix discusses some of the best starting points for free access to laws and court decisions, but surfing the Web will uncover endless additional sources of information. Before you can research the law, however, you must have a basic understanding of the American legal system.

The most important source of law in the United States is the Constitution. Originally enacted in 1787, the Constitution outlines the structure of our federal government, as well as setting limits on the types of laws that the federal government and state governments can enact. Through the centuries, a number of amendments have added to or changed the Constitution, most notably the first 10 amendments, which collectively are known as the "Bill of Rights" and which guarantee important civil liberties.

Reading the plain text of the Constitution provides little information. For example, the Constitution prohibits "unreasonable searches and seizures" by the police. To understand concepts in the Constitution, it is necessary to look to the decisions of the U.S. Supreme Court, which has the ultimate authority in interpreting the meaning of the Constitution. For example, the U.S. Supreme Court's 2001 decision in *Kyllo v. United States* held that scanning the outside of a person's house using a heat sensor to determine whether the person is growing marijuana is an unreasonable search—if it is done without first getting a search warrant from a judge. Each state also has its own constitution and a supreme court that is the ultimate authority on its meaning.

Also important are the written laws, or "statutes," passed by the U.S. Congress and the individual state legislatures. As with constitutional provisions, the U.S. Supreme Court and the state supreme courts are the ultimate authorities in interpreting the meaning of federal and state laws, respectively. However, the U.S. Supreme Court might find that a state law violates the U.S. Constitution, and a state supreme court might find that a state law violates either the state or U.S. Constitution.

Not every controversy reaches either the U.S. Supreme Court or the state supreme courts, however. Therefore, the decisions of other courts are also important. Trial courts hear evidence from both sides and make a decision, while appeals courts review the decisions made by trial courts. Sometimes rulings from appeals courts are appealed further to the U.S. Supreme Court or the state supreme courts.

Lawyers and courts refer to statutes and court decisions through a formal system of citations. Use of these citations reveals which court made the decision or which legislature passed the statute, and allows one to quickly locate the statute or court case online or in a law library. For example, the Supreme Court case *Brown v. Board of Education* has the legal citation 347 U.S. 483 (1954). At a law library, this 1954 decision can be found on page 483 of volume 347 of the U.S. Reports, which are the official collection of the Supreme Court's decisions. On the following page, you will find sample of all the major kinds of legal citation.

Finding sources of legal information on the Internet is relatively simple thanks to "portal" sites such as findlaw.com and lexisone.com, which allow the user to access a variety of constitutions, statutes, court opinions, law review articles, news articles, and other useful sources of information. For example, findlaw.com offers access to all Supreme Court decisions since 1893. Other useful sources of information include gpo.gov, which contains a complete copy of the U.S. Code, and thomas.loc.gov, which offers access to bills pending before Congress, as well as recently passed laws. Of course, the Internet changes every second of every day, so it is best to do some independent searching.

Of course, many people still do their research at law libraries, some of which are open to the public. For example, some state governments and universities offer the public access to their law collections. Law librarians can be of great assistance, as even experienced attorneys need help with legal research from time to time.

Common Citation Forms

Source of Law	Sample Citation	Notes
U.S. Supreme Court	*Employment Division v. Smith*, 485 U.S. 660 (1988)	The U.S. Reports is the official record of Supreme Court decisions. There is also an unofficial Supreme Court ("S. Ct.") reporter.
U.S. Court of Appeals	*United States v. Lambert*, 695 F.2d 536 (11th Cir.1983)	Appellate cases appear in the Federal Reporter, designated by "F." The 11th Circuit has jurisdiction in Alabama, Florida, and Georgia.
U.S. District Court	*Carillon Importers, Ltd. v. Frank Pesce Group, Inc.*, 913 F.Supp. 1559 (S.D.Fla.1996)	Federal trial-level decisions are reported in the Federal Supplement ("F. Supp."). Some states have multiple federal districts; this case originated in the Southern District of Florida.
U.S. Code	Thomas Jefferson Commemoration Commission Act, 36 U.S.C., §149 (2002)	Sometimes the popular names of legislation—names with which the public may be familiar—are included with the U.S. Code citation.
State Supreme Court	*Sterling v. Cupp*, 290 Ore. 611, 614, 625 P.2d 123, 126 (1981)	The Oregon Supreme Court decision is reported in both the state's reporter and the Pacific regional reporter.
State Statute	Pennsylvania Abortion Control Act of 1982, 18 Pa. Cons. Stat. 3203-3220 (1990)	States use many different citation formats for their statutes.

Statutes

Statute of Anne (9 Anne, ch. 14)

This law passed by the English Parliament in 1710 barred the recovery of gambling debts in court. The statute was adopted by U.S. states after the United States won independence. Even today, it remains the law in many states.

Public Law 87-216 (18 U.S.C. §1084), the Interstate Wire Act of 1961 (Wire Act)

This law, originally aimed at bookmakers, makes it a crime to accept bets placed across state lines by telephone. The Wire Act has been used, with some success, by federal authorities in their fight against gambling Web sites.

Public Law 100-497 (25 U.S.C. §§2701–2721), the Indian Gaming Regulatory Act of 1988 (IGRA)

Passed by Congress in response to the *Cabazon* decision, the IGRA set up a framework under which Native American tribes could offer bingo (Class II) and casino-type gaming (Class III) on tribal lands.

Public Law 104-169, the National Gambling Impact Study Commission Act of 1996

This act created the National Gambling Impact Study Commission, a nine-member body that reported its findings and recommendations in 1999.

Public Law 109-347, §§801–803 (31 U.S.C. §§5361–5367), the Unlawful Internet Gambling Enforcement Act of 2006 (UIGEA)

This was the first federal law aimed at online gambling, per se. The UIGEA makes it a crime for an illegal gambling Web site to accept funds from American bettors, and requires financial institutions to take steps to block such transfers.

Cases

California v. Cabazon Band of Mission Indians, 480 U.S. 202 (1987)

Applying the long-standing principle that Native American tribes are sovereign nations, the Supreme Court held that a state has the power to forbid gambling on tribal lands only if that state's laws forbid the same form of gambling everywhere else.

Greater New Orleans Broadcasting Association v. United States, 523 U.S. 173 (1999)

The Supreme Court held that a 1934 federal law restricting gambling-related advertising was unconstitutional with respect to commercial casinos because it was no longer federal policy to discourage gambling and there were alternatives to an outright ban on advertising.

Joker Club v. Hardin, 183 N.C. App. 92, 643 S.E. 2d 626 (Ct. App. 2007)

A state appeals court ruled that poker is a "game of chance" within the meaning of North Carolina's gambling laws. Most court decisions have applied the "predominant factor" test and on that basis have concluded that despite the importance of skill, the outcome of a poker game is largely decided by chance.

Merrill v. Trump Indiana, Inc., 320 F.3d 729 (7th Cir. 2003)

Applying Indiana law, a federal appeals court concluded that a casino was not liable for allowing a compulsive gambler to continue playing even though it was told that he had a gambling problem. In general, a gambler cannot sue a casino that has complied with state gaming rules. A casino that violates the rules must answer to state gaming authorities, not the gambler.

United States v. Cohen, 260 F.3d 68 (2nd Cir. 2001)

A federal appeals court upheld the conviction of an owner of an offshore gambling Web site under the Wire Act. In doing so, the court applied the legal principle that gambling is considered to have occurred both at the location where the bet is placed and the location where it is accepted.

Terms and Concepts

advertising
banking games
bookmaker
compulsive gambling
convenience gambling
destination casinos
federalism
Gamblers Anonymous
games of chance/games of skill
gaming/gambling
house advantage
Indian Gaming Regulatory Act
jurisdiction
Kefauver Commission
laws of probability
lottery
National Gambling Impact Study
    Commission
Nevada Gaming Control Board/
    Nevada Gaming Commission

off-track betting
online gambling
organized crime
pari-mutuel wagering
point shaving
police powers
probability
Prohibition
Protestant work ethic
regressive taxation
self-exclusion
slot machines
sports betting
Statute of Anne
tribal gaming
underage gambling
Unlawful Internet Gaming
    Enforcement Act
victimless crime
Wire Act

INTRODUCTION: Gambling in the United States

1 John W. Weier, ed., *Gambling: What's at Stake?* (Detroit: Thomson Gale, 2007), 1.
2 Robert Goodman, *The Luck Business: The Devastating Consequences and Broken Promises of America's Gambling Explosion* (New York: The Free Press, 1995), 7.
3 Jackson Lears, *Something for Nothing: Luck in America* (New York: Penguin Group, 2003), 86.
4 Richard Hoffer, *Jackpot Nation: Rambling and Gambling Across Our Landscape of Luck* (New York, HarperCollins, 2007), 199.
5 Lears, *Something for Nothing*, 171.
6 *Ibid.*, 195.
7 *Ibid.*, 242.
8 Public Law 100–497, codified as 25 U.S.C. §§2701–2721.
9 25 U.S.C. §2710(d)(1)(B).
10 American Psychiatric Association, *Diagnostic and Statistical Manual of Mental Disorders*, 4th ed. (Washington, DC: American Psychiatric Association, 1994), §312.31.
11 National Gambling Impact and Policy Commission, *The National Gambling Impact Study Commission: final report* (Washington, DC: The Commission, 1999), 1–7.
12 Public Law 87–216, codified as 18 U.S.C. §1084.
13 §§801–803, Public Law 109–347, codified as 31 U.S.C. §§5361–5367

POINT: Gambling Is Harmful to Society

14 United States, *Gambling in America: final report* (Washington, DC: The Commission, 1976), 102.
15 David G. Schwartz, *Roll the Bones: The History of Gambling* (New York: Gotham Books, 2006), 379–380.
16 *The National Gambling Impact Study Commission: final report*, 2–6.
17 Vicki Abt, James F. Smith, and Eugene Martin Christiansen, *The Business of Risk: Commercial Gambling in Mainstream America* (Lawrence: University Press of Kansas, 1985), 159.

18 Jeffrey Kluger, "When Gambling Becomes Obsessive," *Time*, July 25, 2005.
19 Saum is quoted in *The National Gambling Impact Study Commission: final report*, 5.
20 Testimony of prosecuting attorney Jeffrey Bloomberg, Lawrence County, South Dakota, before the House Committee on Small Business, September 21, 1994.
21 Carl G. Bechtold, *Tide of Gambling Yields Backwash of Addiction* (Washington, DC: National Coalition Against Legalized Gambling, 2004), 10.
22 Testimony of Jeffrey Bloomberg.
23 Peter Nicholas, Susan Finch, and Mark Schleifstein are quoted in Goodman, *The Luck Business*, 61.
24 Goodman, *The Luck Business*, 79.
25 Hoffer, *Jackpot Nation*, 154–155.
26 The commission is quoted in Paul Simon, "The Explosive Growth of Gambling in the United States," *Congressional Record*, July 31, 1995.
27 Goodman, *The Luck Business*, 188.
28 Quoted in Simon, "The Explosive Growth of Gambling in the United States."

COUNTERPOINT: Gambling Prohibition Does More Harm Than Good

29 Abt, Smith, and Christiansen, *The Business of Risk*, 1.
30 *Ibid.*, 143.
31 Public Sector Gaming Study Commission, *Gambling Policy and the Role of the State* (Tallahassee: Florida Institute of Government, Florida State University, 2000), 35.
32 *Ibid.*, 37.
33 Schwartz, *Roll the Bones*, 140.
34 Abt, Smith, and Christiansen, *The Business of Risk*, 162–163.
35 Schwartz, *Roll the Bones*, 276.
36 Weier, *Gambling*, 109.
37 Tamara Audi and Adam Thompson, "Oddsmakers in Vegas Play New Sports Role," *The Wall Street Journal*, October 3, 2007.
38 Schwartz, *Roll the Bones*, 140.
39 Lears, *Something for Nothing*, 5.
40 Hoffer, *Jackpot Nation*, 17.

41 Abt, Smith, and Christiansen, *The Business of Risk*, 9.
42 Nick Gillespie, "Wagers of Sin: Dealing with the Anti-Gambling Backlash," *Reason* 28, no. 2 (June 1996): 8.
43 Lears, *Something for Nothing*, 169.
44 Abt, Smith, and Christiansen, *The Business of Risk*, 6.
45 Charles Murray, "The G.O.P.'s Bad Bet," *The New York Times*, October 19, 2006.

POINT: Legalized Gambling Has Adverse Economic and Political Consequences
46 Goodman, *The Luck Business*, 174.
47 *Ibid.*, 167.
48 *The National Gambling Impact Study Commission: final report*, 6–13.
49 Goodman, *The Luck Business*, 18–19.
50 *Ibid.*, 20, 21.
51 Testimony of Jeffrey Bloomberg.
52 *The National Gambling Impact Study Commission: final report*, 7–10.
53 Quoted in John Warren Kindt, "The Negative Impacts of Legalized Gambling on Businesses," *University of Miami Business Law Journal* 4, no. 2 (Spring 1994): 121–122.
54 Kindt, "The Negative Impacts of Legalized Gambling on Businesses," 123–124.
55 *The National Gambling Impact Study Commission: final report*, 1–5.
56 Goodman, *The Luck Business*, 92–93.
57 Hoffer, *Jackpot Nation*, 174.
58 Bloomberg is quoted in Goodman, *The Luck Business*, 93.
59 *Ibid.*, 70.
60 Fong is quoted in Gary Rivlin, "Casinos Go All In to Draw Asians," *The New York Times*, June 13, 2007.
61 Bechtold, *Tide of Gambling Yields Backwash of Addiction*, 2.
62 *The National Gambling Impact Study Commission: final report*, 7–30.
63 §463.368(6), Nevada Revised Statutes.

COUNTERPOINT: Legalized Gaming Benefits States and Communities
64 Hoffer, *Jackpot Nation*, 2.
65 Abt, Smith, and Christiansen, *The Business of Risk*, 14.
66 Schwartz, *Roll the Bones*, 488.

67 Abt, Smith, and Christiansen, *The Business of Risk*, 135.
68 *Ibid.*, 11–12.
69 Benedict Carey, "Lotto Makes Sense, Even for Losers," *The New York Times*, March 11, 2007.
70 *Ibid.*
71 *California v. Cabazon Band of Mission Indians*, 480 U.S. 202, 218–219 (1987).
72 Hoffer, *Jackpot Nation*, 165.
73 *The National Gambling Impact Study Commission: final report*, 6.
74 *Ibid.*, Appendix I, Statement of Robert Loescher.
75 *Ibid.*, 7.
76 *Ibid.*, Appendix I, Statement of John Wilhelm.
77 *The National Gambling Impact Study Commission: final report*, 7–1.
78 Corey Williams, "Detroit Casinos Deliver on Promises of Money and Jobs," *Detroit Free Press*, September 11, 2007.
79 *Ibid.*
80 Michael Rubino, "Town Hopes Casino Brings New Gilded Age," *The New York Times*, October 26, 2006.
81 Leonard A. Blackwell II, "Gaming Post-Katrina: Casinos, Tourism Industry Redefining Future of State's Gulf Coast," *Jackson Clarion-Ledger*, September 9, 2007.

POINT: Government Promotion of Gambling Is Bad Policy
82 *The National Gambling Impact Study Commission: final report*, 3–4.
83 Schwartz, *Roll the Bones*, 369.
84 Ron Stodghill, "The Lottery Industry's Own Powerball," *New York Times*, November 18, 2007.
85 *The National Gambling Impact Study Commission: final report*, 3–4.
86 Hoffer, *Jackpot Nation*, 182.
87 *The National Gambling Impact Study Commission: final report*, 3–16.
88 Quoted in Hoffer, *Jackpot Nation*, 203–204.
89 Goodman, *The Luck Business*, 132.
90 *Ibid.*, 129.
91 *Ibid.*, 164–165.
92 *The National Gambling Impact Study Commission: final report*, 3–19.

93 Goodman, *The Luck Business*, 190–191.
94 *The National Gambling Impact Study Commission: final report*, Appendix I, Statement of Richard C. Leone.
95 Donald E. Miller, "Schools Lose Out in Lotteries," *USA Today*, April 15, 2004.
96 Goodman, *The Luck Business*, 188–189.
97 *Ibid.*, xii.
98 *Ibid.*, 155.

COUNTERPOINT: Government Policy Has Made Gaming Less Harmful
99 Schwartz, *Roll the Bones*, 85.
100 *Ibid.*, 95.
101 Edward M. Brecher, et al., *Licit and Illicit Drugs* (Boston: Little, Brown, 1972), 265–266.
102 Schwartz, *Roll the Bones*, 370–371.
103 *Ibid.*, 419.
104 *The National Gambling Impact Study Commission: final report*, 3–1.
105 American Gaming Association, "Is the Casino Industry Controlled by Mobsters and Organized Crime?" Gaming Industry FAQ, available online, http://www.americangaming.org/industry/faq_detail.cfv?id=64.
106 National Indian Gaming Association, *The Economic Impact of Indian Gaming in 2006* (Washington, DC: National Indian Gaming Association, 2007), 26.
107 American Gaming Association, "Code of Conduct for Responsible Gaming," Responsible Gaming, available online, http://www.americangaming.org/programs/responsiblegaming/code_public.cfm.
108 *Ibid.*
109 North American Association of State and Provincial Lotteries, "NASPL Advertising Guidelines," available online, http://www.naspl.org/index.cfm?fuseaction=content&PageID=39.
110 North American Association of State and Provincial Lotteries, "Did You Know?" available online, http://www.naspl.org/index.cfm?fuseaction=content&PageID=41&PageCategory=38.
111 *Ibid.*
112 Justin Wolfers, "Blow the Whistle on Betting Scandals," *The New York Times*, July 27, 2007.
113 *Ibid.*
114 Schwartz, *Roll the Bones*, 240–241.
115 North American Association of State and Provincial Lotteries, "Did You Know?"
116 *Ibid.*

CONCLUSION: The Future of Legalized Gambling
117 *The National Gambling Impact Study Commission: final report*, 1.
118 Schwartz, *Roll the Bones*, 447.
119 *The National Gambling Impact Study Commission: final report*, Appendix I, Statement of Robert W. Loescher.
120 *Ibid.*, 1–8.
121 *Ibid.*, 1–4.
122 Goodman, *The Luck Business*, 180.
123 Weier, *Gambling*, 5.
124 *Greater New Orleans Broadcasting Association v. United States*, 527 U.S. 173, 187 (1999).
125 Goodman, *The Luck Business*, 183.
126 Public Law 102–559.
127 *The National Gambling Impact Study Commission: final report*, Statement of William A. Bible.
128 Quoted in *The National Gambling Impact Study Commission: final report*, 3–9.
129 *Ibid.*, 2–16.
130 Weier, *Gambling*, 119.
131 American Gaming Association, "Internet Gambling," Fact Sheet on Gaming Industry Issues, available online, http://www.americangaming.org/Industry/factsheets/issues_detail.cfv?id=17.
132 Hoffer, *Jackpot Nation*, 233.

Abt, Vicki, James F. Smith, and Eugene Martin Christiansen. *The Business of Risk: Commercial Gambling in Mainstream America*. Lawrence: University Press of Kansas, 1985.

American Psychiatric Association. *Diagnostic and Statistical Manual of Mental Disorders*. 4th ed. Washington, D.C.: American Psychiatric Association, 1994.

Goodman, Robert. *The Luck Business: The Devastating Consequences and Broken Promises of America's Gambling Explosion*. New York: The Free Press, 1995.

National Gambling Impact and Policy Commission. *The National Gambling Impact Study Commission: final report*. Washington, D.C.: The Commission, 1999.

Schwartz, David G. *Roll the Bones: The History of Gambling*. New York: Gotham Books, 2006.

Web Sites
Organizations
The American Gaming Association
http://www.americangaming.org
> AGA is the trade association that represents the nation's commercial casinos. The association believes that adults should be able to gamble legally and argues in favor of legalization. The AGA has adopted a voluntary code of conduct for responsible gaming.

Gamblers Anonymous
http://www.gamblersanonymous.org
> GA is a fellowship of people with gambling problems who try to help one another recover. It does not engage in political activity, but does believe that those who do have a problem must abstain from gambling in order to recover.

The Institute for Problem Gambling
http://www.gamblingproblem.net
> This organization was created in 1997 to further the study, prevention, and treatment of gambling problems. It sponsors symposiums and training programs for professionals, especially those in the treatment field.

The National Coalition Against Legalized Gambling
http://www.ncalg.org
> The NCALG is an organization that attempts to educate policymakers by providing them with information about the harmful effects of gambling. Its sister organization, the National Coalition Against Gambling Expansion (www.ncage.org), is dedicated to political action.

The National Indian Gaming Association
http://www.indiangaming.org
The NIGA is an organization of Native American groups that offer gaming on their land. The association believes that tribal gaming should remain legal because revenue from bingo and casinos makes Native Americans more self-sufficient and improves their quality of life.

The North American Association of State and Provincial Lotteries
http://www.naspl.org
This is a trade association that represents more than 50 government-run lotteries in the United States and Canada. Its functions include ensuring that games are run fairly and marketed in a responsible manner.

Government Agencies and Regulatory Bodies
The National Indian Gaming Commission
http://www.nigc.gov.
The NIGC is a federal agency created by the IGRA. It is responsible for overseeing gaming on tribal lands. The NIGC has the power to bar undesirables, investigate tribal gaming operations, and penalize violators of the IGRA.

The Nevada Gaming Control Board and Nevada Gaming Commission
http://gaming.nv.gov
This is a two-tiered regulatory structure that is responsible for regulating the nation's largest gaming economy. It was created during the late 1950s and has served as a model for other states that allow gaming. The board and commission license those involved in the industry, collect taxes and fees, and adopt and enforce gaming rules.

The United States Justice Department
http://www.usdoj.gov
Part of the executive branch, this department is responsible for enforcing federal laws, including those related to sports and Internet betting in particular, and organized crime in general.

Gambling Law Resources
Gambling and the Law
http://www.gamblingandthelaw.com
Gambling and the Law is a Web site maintained by Professor I. Nelson Rose, an expert on gambling law. It contains a number of articles that offer Rose's analysis of legal issues related to gambling.

PAUL RUSCHMANN, J.D., is a legal analyst and writer based in Canton, Michigan. He received his undergraduate degree from the University of Notre Dame and his law degree from the University of Michigan. He is a member of the State Bar of Michigan. His areas of specialization include legislation, public safety, traffic and transportation, and trade regulation. He is the author of 10 other books in the POINT/COUNTERPOINT series, which deal with such issues as the War on Terror, the military draft, indecency in the media, prescription and non-prescription drugs, and private property rights. He can be found online at www.PaulRuschmann.com.

ALAN MARZILLI, M.A., J.D., lives in Birmingham, Alabama, and is a program associate with Advocates for Human Potential, Inc., a research and consulting firm based in Sudbury, Massachusetts, and Albany, New York. He primarily works on developing training and educational materials for agencies of the federal government on topics such as housing, mental health policy, employment, and transportation. He has spoken on mental health issues in 30 states, the District of Columbia, and Puerto Rico; his work has included training mental health administrators, nonprofit management and staff, and people with mental illnesses and their families on a wide variety of topics, including effective advocacy, community-based mental health services, and housing. Marzilli has written several handbooks and training curricula that are used nationally and as far away as the U.S. territory of Guam. Additionally, he managed statewide and national mental health advocacy programs and worked for several public interest lobbying organizations while studying law at Georgetown University. Marzilli has written more than a dozen books, including numerous titles in the POINT/COUNTERPOINT series.

PICTURE CREDITS |||||▷

PAGE

17: AP Images/Carrie Osgood
60: AP Images/Mark Humphrey
67: AP Images/Dawn Armato-Brehm

78: AP Images
97: AP Images/Lennox Mclendon
121: AP Images/Santilli

mb   6/09